A
MAINE YANKEE
AT HOME AND ABROAD
1903–1916

The Journals and Logs of Robert Hale

STANDISH MEACHAM

$\mathscr{A}$ MAINE YANKEE
AT HOME AND ABROAD
1903–1916

The Journals and Logs of Robert Hale

STANDISH MEACHAM

A MAINE YANKEE AT HOME AND ABROAD 1903–1916
THE JOURNALS AND LOGS OF ROBERT HALE

iUniverse books may be ordered through booksellers or by contacting:

iUniverse
1663 Liberty Drive
Bloomington, IN 47403
www.iuniverse.com
1-800-Authors (1-800-288-4677)

ISBN: 978-1-5320-3851-8 (sc)
ISBN: 978-1-5320-3852-5 (e)

Front cover photo: Robert Hale at the helm, 1909.
Map by Jim Anderson

Print information available on the last page.

iUniverse rev. date: 04/12/2018

For Sarah Meacham
Steadfast voyager

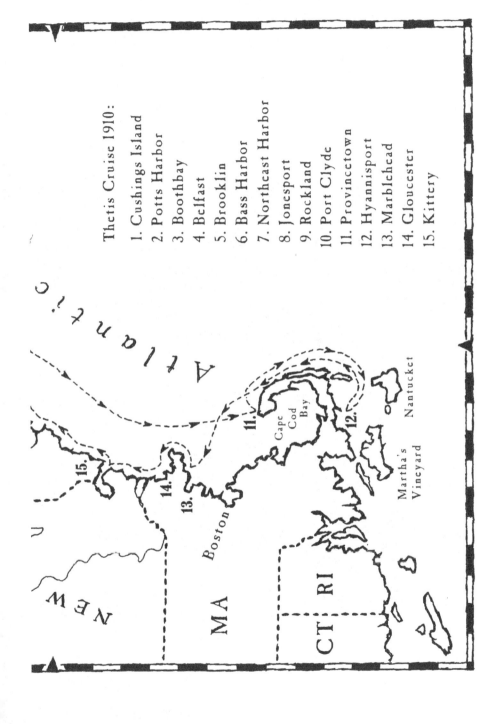

Thetis Cruise 1910:

1. Cushings Island
2. Potts Harbor
3. Boothbay
4. Belfast
5. Brooklin
6. Bass Harbor
7. Northeast Harbor
8. Jonesport
9. Rockland
10. Port Clyde
11. Provincetown
12. Hyannisport
13. Marblehead
14. Gloucester
15. Kittery

Contents

Contents

Foreword

"Before all and through all, I must be a seaman."

So Robert Hale declared, when seventeen years old. Born in Portland, Maine in 1889, he had spent all but the first two summers of his life in his family's cottage on Cushings Island in Casco Bay. His journals and ship logs, kept when he was sailing the coast and while he was a Rhodes Scholar at Oxford before the First World War, show him to have been a gifted young observer and writer, with a sense of himself anchored in the sea and rooted in the seacoast he knew and celebrated.

Robert was the son of Clarence Hale, lawyer and U.S. District Judge, and Margaret Rollins Hale. He was the nephew of Eugene Hale and cousin of Frederick Hale, both Maine senators. Educated at Portland private and public schools, he entered Bowdoin College in 1906. Following graduation in 1910, he attended Trinity College, Oxford as a Rhodes Scholar for two years, where he read for a BA in law. He remained at Oxford for a third year of legal studies and European travel. On his return to the U.S. he enrolled in Harvard Law School. Following graduation, he practiced law in Boston and Portland, prior to service as a junior officer in France during the World War. Shortly after the Armistice he was appointed to the American Commission to negotiate peace in the Baltic.

During the long period from 1920 until retirement in 1975 he continued practicing law in Portland and Washington, D.C. From 1923 to 1930 he served as a Republican in the Maine House of Representatives, with one term as Speaker in 1929-30. Throughout his political career in the twenties he was an outspoken opponent of the Ku Klux Klan's repeated campaigns to deny all state aid to parochial schools, attacking Maine Klan leader Eugene Farnsworth as "an ignorant demagogue", and comparing the Klan's activities to attempts to stifle the teaching of German during the First World War and the teaching of evolution in Tennessee in the twenties.

Hale was elected to the U.S. Congress in 1942. Though an outspoken opponent of the New Deal, he supported Roosevelt's internationalist foreign policy. During the Cold War, however, he veered to the right, attacking Truman's firing of General Douglas MacArthur at the height of the Korean War and supporting, at least for a time, the self-proclaimed campaign of Senator Joseph McCarthy to rid the country of Communists. His attempt to have Truman impeached following the president's nationalization of the steel industry got nowhere.

Hale lost his reelection campaign in 1958 after eight terms in the House. Though he did not retire from the law until 1975, he spent increasing amounts of time in Portland and on Cushings Island with his wife, Agnes Burke Hale. He died the day after his eighty-seventh birthday on November 30, 1976. (*Lewiston Daily Sun*, March 22, 1923; *Lewiston Evening Journal*, March 24, 1923; *Lewiston Daily Sun*, April 8, 1950; *Portsmouth Times*, April 22, 1952)

Most of the story of Hale's life as a boy and young man is contained in the sixteen notebooks which he kept from 1902 to 1920. Six are diaries and journals entitled "Some Impressions and Events". They include an account of the nine-month European grand tour that he, his mother, and his older sister made in 1902-1903; occasional essays, poems, and observations written throughout his boyhood and youth; and the detailed history of his three years at Oxford. The remaining volumes are meticulously kept annual ship logs of Hale's day sails and cruises in his boats: Mermaid, a twenty-six foot sloop his parents commissioned in 1902, and the much larger sloop Thetis which he was given in 1907. I have arranged the notebooks in roughly chronological order, volumes I-XVI, and refer to them as such in the text.

I have spent summers on Cushings Island since the late 1950's and was fortunate to have known Robert Hale in his later years, an erudite, witty gentleman, though someone who did not suffer fools. I first had a look at the journals and logs following Agnes Hale's death in the early 1980's. I was struck then by their importance as historical documents and by the grace and power of Hale's prose and poetry, impressive, especially, in someone so young. More than once, I imagined a book derived from the material. I am now pleased to have been given the chance to write such a book by Howard Dana, Hale's great-nephew, who possesses his personal papers.

In a memoir published with his wife at the end of his life, Hale recalled at length his summers on Cushings Island. About his annual cruises, however, he said only this: "When I was 13, I was allowed to have a twenty-six foot sailboat, and for the next ten years I was mostly waterborne. We sailed up and down the New England coast from Campobello to Hyannis, but that is another story." (Robert Hale, "Cushings Island: A Memoir", ca. 1970, 28. Hereafter cited as CIM.)

This is that story. It tells of a young man who created a

world for himself, conceived from romantic notions of past and present and reflecting an innocence derived from America's new-world isolation from the complexities and cynicisms of the old. While touring the Continent in the spring of 1913, Hale went to inspect a set of recently installed generators – he calls them dynamos – in France. He saw them as the harbingers of a better future for mankind, declaring that, terrifying though they might seem, they promised "a world of order, a rebuke to the chaotic, the noisy, the disorderly, the dirty." (RH XVI, 118-19)

Yet Hale would soon find himself, with the rest of his generation of Americans, in the midst of the most chaotic, noisy, disorderly, and dirty conflict the world had ever witnessed. For him, as for so many, the war would compel a struggle with the past that they had so painstakingly and lovingly created for themselves. When the war seized upon that past and tried to rip it from those men, how fierce was the ensuing struggle? And when they began their post-war lives, how much of that past did they still carry with them? Whatever the answers to those questions, knowledge of that created past remains essential to an understanding of both pre- and post-war years. Because Hale's evocative writings carry us toward that knowledge, I believe they are well worth bringing to light.

Standish Meacham

Sailing The Coast

Early Years

In October of 1906, a month shy of turning seventeen and a newly arrived freshman at Bowdoin College, Robert Hale took time to set down "Some Events and Recollections of My Life." (All quotations that follow in this section are taken from RH IV, through 1906, and RH V, from 1907 forward.) He begins, in characteristic manner, at once self-satisfied and yet self-doubting. "On November 29, 1889, I was born into the Hale family. This incident I have never regretted and I am sure that if my future environment had been left to me, I should not have made so good a choice."

He proceeds to catalogue the mundane events of his infancy and early childhood: the comfortable, contented life he led with his father, mother, and older sister Katharine, in a three-story house on the fashionable Western Promenade in Portland. He does pause long enough to report that an event of "great importance in its consequences" occurred in the summer of 1892, "when [my family] took up residence on Cushings Island, Casco Bay.... It is here that my happiest days have been spent, and for fourteen years this island has been a perfect mine of almost pure joy."

Since the 1860s, Cushings Island, only a few miles and

twenty minutes by ferry from downtown Portland, had enjoyed increasing popularity as a summer resort. Though developed by Lemuel Cushing, a Canadian, and his two sons Francis and Thomas, the island took its name from a much earlier distant Cushing forebear, Ezekiel, who built himself a house there in the 1760s. The latter-day Cushings were prepared to spend money to ensure the success of their venture. They opened their first hotel, the Ottawa House, in 1862, and a second, grander version a generation later. They hired Frederick Law Olmsted to lay out plans for the island's future development. And they encouraged those to whom they sold property to engage first-rate architects to design their cottages for them – most notably John Calvin Stevens of Portland, a well-regarded practitioner of the Shingle Style. Though at first most vacationers came from Canada, by the end of the century a number of Portlanders summered there, as well as families from as far away as St. Louis and Chicago.

Before the beginning of their third season, the Hales bought the cottage of a local artist, Will Sargent, and hired Stevens to design a large addition. In his later memoir Hale wrote toward the end of his life, he had a good time describing the house that was to be the seat of his pleasurable summer existence for the next twenty years.

I never knew Will Sargent, at least I have no memory of ever having seen him. He was a man of literary tastes, for over the mantels…were various inscriptions carved or on tiles. The inscriptions are still there and worth quoting. In the dining room, lines from Shakespeare's "Cymbeline":

> Laud we the gods. And let our crooked smokes
> Climb to their nostrils
> From our blessed altars

In the living room a Latin maxim, "Fumus noster igne alieno luculentior," which freely translated means "We prefer our smoke to our neighbor's fire…." Few men today would carve poems or mottoes over their fireplaces. It would be thought pretentious or affected. But there they are today, and I salute Will Sargent. (CIM, 10.)

In his earlier, teen-age recollections, Hale records his increasing attraction to the sea. By 1897 he was rowing and sailing regularly, though always accompanied by an adult, since he had not yet learned to swim. The year before, he recalls experiencing for the first time "the romance of the Maine waters, the sheen of the far-surrounding seas" on a trip with the family's manservant in a steamer to Yarmouth, Maine. Each year he spent more and more of his time on the water. "In 1899, the greatest event of the season proved to be my trip with my aunt to Damariscotta. This fired my desires to explore still farther the bays and inlets of the Maine coast….I had always been interested in maps and especially nautical charts, but now I began constantly to increase my collection."

By 1900 he was taking sailing lessons from his uncle in a catboat. His inability to swim continued to prevent him from setting forth on his own. Not until the summer of 1901 was he free to rove the Bay alone. From his later memoir: "I discovered that by moving my arms and legs rather rapidly, I could keep afloat and I later learned a certain amount of control over my thrashing members. Not until the 'thirties did I try to acquire anything like form." (CIM, 6)

In 1898 the family acquired a rowboat, christened Constance, and it was aboard her that Hale now spent most of his waking summer hours. It was not as an oarsman, however, but as a sailor that he dreamed of making his mark. The following year, he began to realize that dream.

One bright morning in the latter part of June I recognized the sails of the Lottie W [a sloop owned and captained by George Randall, who lived on next-door Peaks Island, and took hotel guests and cottagers for day-sailing trips] and going to the wharf I saw George and another man sitting in the cockpit.

This man was Lon Randall [Alonzo, George's brother]. I had no realization at the time of the friendship which should grow up between us and his relation to my life. For in spite of the fact that he was fifty years my senior I was with him most of the time that summer and for that matter, many others. Almost every day George and Lon took a party from the Ottawa House and almost as often I went with them. During these sails I learned much. I became thoroughly acquainted with the rigging fore and aft, learned every knot known to nautical science, and besides all this had many practical lessons in actual sailing.

My education therefore in this special branch was as good as could be had in any part of the world at any price. Two years with my uncle gave me considerable knowledge of the theory and practice of the great art of sailing and navigation. A course after that with two great masters made me competent to command my own craft. And there is no doubt that these men were masters. For the one [George] was a professional fisherman of thirty years experience while the other had been coasting and off shore to the West Indies for hard on to sixty.

It was during this year that I made my trip to Monhegan with the rest of the family on the Lottie W. [It] lingers in the mind of every one of us as one of the pleasantest memories of our lives. The weather was perfect, the waters and lands charmed us with their beauty and novelty, and the society of George and Lon was an unending joy. Their quaintness of expression and conscious and unconscious wit was such that for hours I listened with unfailing interest.

During the summer of 1902, Hale had been sailing Constance, rigged by Lon with a mast and tiny leg-of-mutton sail. Yet his newly acquired skills called for something more sea-worthy. The next summer following a Grand Tour of Europe with his mother and sister, he was presented with a twenty-six foot sloop, Mermaid, designed and built to Lon's specifications over the winter.

On June 16, for the first time I saw Mermaid. She had just come from the shop, planked and sealed but lacking six weeks of completion. Lon had built [it] four feet longer than the original plan thus giving ample cabin accommodations for two and a large cockpit. She was the best built I had ever (I might say have ever) seen. She was built on the model of the fastest, ablest fisherman (of her size) out of Gloucester and she afterwards made good the record claimed for her and on many a bay showed her heels to anything of her size....

By August [she] was rigged, equipped and ready for sea with all necessary provisions aboard and Lon and I sailed on what was destined to be a most successful cruise to Bar Harbor.

The following summer saw a second, equally successful cruise with Mermaid. In the fall, Hale entered his junior year at Portland High School, recording with satisfaction that on November 29, 1904 his fifteenth birthday, he for the first time donned long trousers.

His memoir entries for the following two years are brief. He takes note of his sister Katharine's engagement and subsequent marriage to a fellow Portlander, Philip Clifford, and their establishment in a cottage of their own on Cushings Island. During his senior year he took preliminary entrance exams for Bowdoin College, served as business manager of his school newspaper, and joined a fraternity. And again, "the summer was spent in continual sail." Another cruise on Mermaid took him, Lon and a friend Down East to Belfast and back.

On September 27, 1906 he entered Bowdoin. On September 30 – in his estimation a far more auspicious date – "occurred the momentous interview with Mr. Adams, boat builder of East Boothbay. And on October 2 the big boat afterwards named Thetis [in classical mythology a sea nymph and mother of the Greek hero Achilles] was decided upon as a certainty." Though this is Hale's first mention of a "big boat," it must have been a dream of some years: a sloop large enough to test his skills as a mature sailor and to carry him, Lon, and three or four friends on longer summer cruises. Since Hale's mother, Margaret, was a constant passenger on day sails when Thetis was moored in Cushings Cove, it was almost certainly as much her dream as it was her son's. True or not, the senior Hales' willingness to underwrite the cost of a boat twice as big as Mermaid, not to mention an annual summer salary for Lon Randall, was testament both to their ready willingness to indulge their son's nautical ambitions, and to their considerable financial means to see that those ambitions came true.

In a second volume of "Some Impressions and Events" begun in the winter of 1907, Hale wrote regularly of his growing excitement about this boat that would soon be his, and of his dedication to the dream of a lifetime of sailing.

March 5, 1907. Salem, Gloucester, Marblehead, Nantucket, New Bedford, Baltimore, Boston, Portland, Provincetown, Plymouth, Portsmouth, Bath, and New London, these little towns from Maine to Florida, with what tales you may thrill us, of "Dreadnaught" and "Flying Cloud", of clipper, whales, and fishermen, spices of India and the Orient, the pursuit of giant game in Arctic and Antarctic, ceaseless battle from Georges to Salvador, what men and what vessels these were in those glorious days and what may we not expect again in the years to come? I am proud of my country and my lineage and my passion. I will be a student or lawyer or I care not what but before all and through all I must be a seaman.

May 19, 1907. The spring has come at last and Thetis lies at the mooring shining in new paint and rigging and eager to push her great spike bowsprit into the heaving Atlantic. But during the brief remaining period of land work and expectation there is a practice that gives me great comfort. Every evening, when our meal is done, I go seven miles just to sit on the shore and look out on the sea and think of times past and times which, God willing, are to come. But merely to look out on the ocean is an inspiration, a stimulus, physical, mental, and moral. "Down to the sea covers all history," someone has said. It is the most venerable, yet the most novel thing in all nature. Boundless it has been called and boundless it is too…. The very water which laps so gently over the clam flats of Maquoit rages amid the gales of the five oceans and reaches from coral banks of the Pacific to the undiscovered poles. Infinity of time and space are not to be thought of without real reverence. And so to look thoughtfully out over the sea seems to me to be an event full of meaning in my life.

July 1, 1907. Is it not wonderful that in the sight of some old picture comes flooding back upon us the memories of years? I was hastily looking through a book of Cushings Island photographs this evening when I saw one that made me stop and think. It was the cove – the cove as my earliest recollection shows it with all the craft that I first knew. How all the changes that the years bring came to me then. How the time when I first rowed and sailed in those little waters filled my mind with the fondest of memories. For there is no place to which one looks with the same affection as the little cove where first he sailed his boat before the greater mystery of the ocean was made known to him; and to me this cove, identified with much of the happiness of my life, seems in the truest sense my home.

But one thing there is more potent than picture or printed page. It is the odor – the odor of the sea – the odor which is the very quintessence of life itself. It came to me a little later from the sea beach, made the blood run quicker and the heart throb and the nerves tingle, stirring me with a memory whose very fondness is sadness but filling me with a greater hope and noble ambition for the future.

On April 13, Thetis was launched from an East Boothbay shipyard. Hale was not present – presumably detained by some business at Bowdoin, though it is hard to imagine what could have been so pressing a matter as to keep him from being on hand. He was represented by Lon and by a friend, Sumner Fogg, who was to sail as crew on Thetis's maiden cruise. The boat was towed to Portland for rigging. On Memorial Day weekend, Hale, Lon, his brother George, and eight others, including Mrs. Hale, sailed out into Casco Bay for a maiden voyage.

Good time was made all the way, and all feel confident that Thetis is as fast as she is able. For several hours she swung across the Bay at a fine even gait throwing a bit of spray now and then when R. Hale, who was at the wheel, let her roll down and take it extra hard….Luncheon was served on the large table in the after cabin and was heartily appreciated by all the guests….On the way home the Captain and Mate [Hale and Fogg] sat on the footropes and made arrangements for the future. As a whole the sail was pleasant and valuable as proving the noble qualities which may be summarized as the magnified counterparts of Mermaid's.

From that moment forward, for the next seven years, through the summer of 1914, Hale and Thetis were inseparable from late May into September. Whether day-sailing with a party of young ladies and gents from Cushings Island and Portland, racing against boats owned by other islanders, including his brother-in-law Philip Clifford, or cruising Down East as far as Bar Harbor and southwest to Gloucester and Marblehead, Hale was living the life his romantic soul craved: "before all and through all," the life of a sailor.

The Mermaid Cruises, 1903-1906

(From "Brief account of a trip to Bar Harbor made in the year 1903". This description based on memory – and notes, presumably – was written in May 1906, when Hale was sixteen and in his senior year at Portland High School. RH I, 23ff.)

Three years have now gone by since I left for the first and most successful cruise Mermaid ever made: Before, I had made three cruises to the Eastward, but this [was] the first... voyage of any length; and then for the first time I was sailing on my own responsibility in my own boat. ["Captain" Hale aged thirteen, was accompanied by "skipper" Lon Randall].

August 1, 1903. Mermaid, two weeks old, child that she was, swung at her moorings on that bright morning as if conscious of the important voyage that lay before her. She was stocked with provisions, garments and nautical gear sufficient for the comforts of the trip.... At 11 o'clock Lon and I dropped the buoy and waving to our friends on shore, left the [Cushings Island] cove. Mermaid gained speed with the freshening wind, and soon we rounded Cellar Point, jogged lazily out White Head channel and gradually as it "breezed on" the commanding promontory of White Head we [felt] less and less movement over the lengthening waters. And now with a good sou'west wind at our backs we covered the distance lying between Cushings and Small Point, the twenty miles of bays and inlets which have so long been known as Casco Bay.

And what a sail that is! I have beat across the bay when the crested gray waves rose huge ahead and rolled far away astern and the sky was lowering and the wind howled, I have idly drifted by these magic isles in drowsy moments and I have sped away over rippling leagues of sunny waters but always there is an irresistible beauty, a wonderful fascination in the open unobstructed ocean unknown to those who go through the island channels.

The green islands shone in the hot August air and the sparkling sun paths glowed and shimmered with a divine refulgence. The islands lay before us. Let us look at the view from Halfway Rock. Cape Elizabeth lies blue and faint on the western horizon, the highlands of Small P[oin]t show clearer in the east. South lies the sea shining clear and blue with all the glory of the sky above. And north are hundreds of islands merging into one great stretch of projecting retreating green.

But no matter where our travels, our pleasure depends almost wholly on our companions. In view of this then, Lon's society meant everything. For hours we would sail on with only an occasional word. First I was at the tiller and he would busy himself about the dinner or he would steer and I would work out courses, busy myself with some odd task or merely drink in the beauties of the day. Or again I would ask and he would tell me a long lifetime's experiences, … of passages to the Indies, to Oporto or the perils of the coaster and many a fight for life in the fishing boats "lobsterin" or "draggin". But always he was the same: never angry, never irritable, for he had had the education of the sea.

Small Point was past and we crossed Sheepscot Bay, rounded Cape Newagen, traversed Fisherman's Island Passage, crossed Muscongus Bay, sailed through Davis Straits and anchored [at] about six in Port Clyde after 53 miles glorious sail.…

It was cold that night, and the way we lit the stove, closed the doors, had our cozy meal, talked awhile and for the first time in the history of Mermaid turned in, will ever be a subject of fond memories.

August 2, 1903. The sight of the harbor in the early morning was one never to be forgotten. It was enough to make the most confirmed sluggard early leave his downy couch. There is a brilliancy in the atmosphere just at dawn that we never see at any other time or season. Every object in the landscape stands out with crystal clearness. The tiny village, the harbor filled with fishing boats, the picturesque docks, the black evergreens of Marshall's Point in this early light formed a landscape of unique beauty. It was thus that I instantly fell in love with Port Clyde and through many visits my liking for the quaint little village has constantly increased.

Our next stopping place was North Haven Island where we arrived at noon, sailing on after lunch into Penobscot Bay. When one passes Owl's Head the prospect is marvelous. West Penobscot Bay opens up before you from Rockland to Belfast and Owl's Head to Fox Island, dominated by the hills of Camden and lighted that day by the brilliance of a summer sun. With the "sequens ventris" we had that day, however, we speedily crossed the bay and plunged into the narrow and crooked stream of water known as Fox Island thorofare....

When fairly out into the middle of the bay the wind left altogether. But we were well rewarded for this inconvenience, for it [was] our privilege to gaze on a scene of rare beauty. Sunset over the Camden Hills, and the full moon rose from the eastern waters. And as the golden sunset glow faded from the west, the silver light of the moon climbed the eastern sky and lit [the] waters with its magic light. Now and then a fresh breath of air rustled through the sails.... [They proceed on to Mt. Desert and then Bar Harbor]

August 4.... My recollections of the town are not especially pleasant. The harbor affords bad shelter, is generally crowded and is on the whole a disagreeable anchorage. The town itself is not in any degree interesting nor even pretty and at that time of year did not even appear to be especially gay. The country around, however, is delightful, a rare combination of sea and hill.... [As they head for home, the weather turns foul.]

August 6. The wind was S.E., the sky portended rain and the fog lay thick outside. The sea was very heavy – "nasty, stinking, thundering, rotting lousy old sea" was the way Lon spoke of it.

After a couple of desultory entries, and having established the importance to him of this first cruise, Hale abandoned his account before describing his no doubt triumphal return to Cushings Island.

(From "Recollections of a Trip to the East'ard", in the summer of 1904; written by Hale in April, 1906. Hale was accompanied aboard Mermaid by Lon Randall and a friend Tom Bosworth. RH IV, 325 ff.)

July 4, 1904. We occupied the morning in putting aboard all that had not been stowed away the day before, provisions, wraps, bags, water, tools, in short everything that could make three people comfortable for three weeks in a 26 foot boat.... We dropped the mooring buoy overboard, made all plain sail, and in due time arrived at Peak's Island. Lon had characteristically forgotten the potatoes, went ashore and was gone about half an hour in which time the wind freshened into something more worthy of the name of wind. At quarter of twelve Lon returned. We kept off and put the jib topsail on her, thus making good time down the bay.... At about this time, dinner was served on deck. Passenger Bosworth made some objection to using the same knife for corned beef as for butter but was shown the error of his ways [Threatening weather then compelled them to put in at Mackeral Cove on the south end of Bailey's Island, about twelve miles from Portland.]

Mackeral Cove is a fair harbor for anything but a sou'wester... At the northern end...Mermaid hove to and anchored. Tom and I went ashore when all had been made snug alow and aloft. Lon stayed aboard and fixed the awning and hammock on deck [where he was to sleep; presumably, Hale and Bosworth occupied the two bunks.] At six we had supper and at nine or ten we retired, passing a very comfortable night, with the exception of a few mosquitoes.

Thursday, July 7. At four o'clock we got up the anchor and sped away under two oars, the mainsail and jib. The oars did more good than all the sail we could get on her. It is about eight miles from Bailey's Island to Small Point, eight of the most beautiful miles in any part of the world. You can look far up into Quahog Bay and almost see Carter's Cove, which I firmly believe to be the most sequestered, little heard of, and altogether delightful place in the world.

There are not five people in Portland...that have ever heard of it. You can see that mass of ledges to the north, the only reminder that this is not a place of perfect peace, that on certain occasions this would be the most undesirable place in the world to be in.... Many cross this bay, but few take the trouble to go up into what I consider the most beautiful part of the Maine coast.

There are no yachts, no summer cottages, no casinos, no parks or summer theatres here. The typical New England farmhouse with its green blinds is the only type of building seen. The fishermen are the only boats that go up into these lonely bays, and forests of spruce, fir, pine, and cedar are the parks that make this bay delightful....

[Rough seas result in "unpleasantness to Tom's organs"; the decision is reached, therefore, to put in at Boothbay for the night.] Boothbay is not only one of the finest harbors in the Atlantic Seaboard, but it is also without exception the most disagreeable town in the world. The houses are cheap summer cottages mostly. The "Rusticators" [summer people] are of the poorest class and the natives are disagreeable. This is enough to keep one from going ashore there. But in addition there are so many gasoline boats and steamers that even the sea is uncomfortable and crowded.

In the evening we went to the sardine factory, where Lon had friends. There were two magnificent vessels there, two seiners from Gloucester and Cape Porpoise. They had been traveling of late but had had bad luck.

Friday, July 8. The sun rose in all its glory and we with it. But alas, there was no wind. We got started about eleven o'clock, however, having spent the first of the morning with a friend of Lon's on the [vessel] Modoc. We beat out of the harbor and kept off for Ram Island. The breeze freshened, the water became dark blue, and Mermaid for the first time in the trip was bowling right along at six or eight knots. We piled all possible sail on her and watched the water jump away from the bow. Pemaquid was soon passed, and then we had all the glorious vistas of Muscongus Bay to feast our eyes on....

The bay of Naples is the only bay in the world outside of Maine that is to be compared with it in respect to natural scenery. Yes but, someone says, the charm of the bay of Naples is not all scenery. It is the Italian sun, and the romance of Italian life that makes the bay of Naples fascinating. This is true, but the inhabitants of this part of the Maine coast are as truly foreigners and far more romantic ones, than the modern Italians.... [Hale surveys the islands of the bay.] To the south lies Monhegan, the most historic island in America, the Capri of this American Bay of Naples.... [He continues on, ending with the Camden Hills.] What are the high blue hills to the northeast? They are the Vesuviuses of the bay. The Camden Hills are not so high as Vesuvius, nor are they smoking...but they are just high enough to be grand and just low enough to be beautiful.

[They sail to Port Clyde, which had so charmed Hale the previous year.] In the afternoon we hired a steam launch for a trip to Friendship... On one of the islands we passed lives a man with his twelve children, most of whom are married. This must be an interesting brotherhood, living on an island so distant from civilization.

That night in Port Clyde was one to be remembered. Tom and I went ashore late. It was pitch dark. There was no moon. The water was undisturbed by the slightest ripple. There was no sound. The spirit of Peace seemed brooding over the waters. Each drop was a glowing light. The oars were brilliant with phosphorescence. The light in the water danced about in a weird way and the stars in heaven seemed to send back their messages. Truly it is such [nights] as this that awaken all that is noblest in man's soul.

[The following day, July 9, on to Little Deer Isle, and the next to Northeast Harbor, through the "curiously formed channel" of Eggamoggin Reach.] The shores are green and fertile. Huge farms dot the banks on the mainland, the island shores are wilder.... We arrived at Northeast Harbor about five, the fog at six. It is a most remarkable place. The "rusticators" have built palatial summer cottages in the woods, [so] only their chimney tops can be seen.... The year-round residents ...make the best of money out of the summer people, and I was told that bananas were often sold for a dollar....

[Fogged in for two days at nearby Southwest Harbor, Mermaid's crew set sail for the village of Harrington, Lon Randall's birthplace.]

July 14. Our first call was at the Fryes. Mrs Frye was a lovely woman, the wife of the captain that Lon had sailed under as mate for many years. They reminisced.... The house was a typical country house, hospitable and cozy....

July 15. At the turn of the tide we set out in the tender, leaving Mermaid behind for a rest. We stopped at the two-masted coaster Marcia Berkley to talk with Cap'n Ed Frye. That gentleman thinks that Rube Mitchell is a fool to cart sail onto his vessel coming up the river when she's loaded so deep with coal. Rube has been with him many times. The row up to Harrington is about three miles, very pretty ones too. The banks of the river are green and the glimpses of Harrington as it approaches are beautiful....

Harrington used, in the palmy days, to be a big shipbuilding town. Lon has seen twelve vessels built there in one season, and Mr. Hook the sail-master says that from his shop window, he could see nothing but vessels' masts and hear nothing but hammers. It is a decayed old town now with a deserted and sleepy appearance in its streets.

In the center of the town is its "Place d'Armes" [Hale had recently returned from his tour of Europe], the center of activity. On it face the post office, a grocery store, the undertaker's shop, and the station agent's house. From the south side runs the road to one of the wharves. On the east there is the bridge, above which the river is always fordable, and below which only at low tide. To the west leads the main street of the metropolis, with the Methodist and Universalist churches, the main grocery store, the Inn, and the best residences of the town. At the end of the street another and more pretentious bridge crosses the river. The school, Baptist church, and parson's house lie to the east of the first bridge. We stopped at Mrs. Cole's who lives in the grocery store, or rather right above it.

In the afternoon she introduced us to her brother and we started for the "barrens" with him in a carriage. We drove along lovely country roads bordered by a thick growth of trees....In what must have been an hour we arrived at the top of the hill ... and burst upon a view whose equal it would be hard to find. The sea lay sparkling to the south studded with islands and flecked with sails. Seen over miles of intervening tree tops, the little village of Harrington. The Mount Desert hills ... tower in the west, the miles of waving tree tops stretching to the east as far as the eye can see....

The barrens are a desolate plateau of great extent, thirty by thirty miles, perhaps. These plains are productive of nothing but blueberries, but they are so thick that their picking and cleaning give occupation to hundreds of souls. Although it was not the season, we gathered a quart in no time....

July 16. The morning was spent in walks about the town with Lon, and the purchase of cloth for a gaff tops'l to the boat. In the afternoon Mrs. Cole introduced us to a boy called Roby Coffin and we all went to walk in the woods.... Suddenly out of a little clearing a deer who had not been aware of our coming started at a bound and was gone almost before [we] saw him. This will serve to illustrate the wildness of the country....

July 18, [Mermaid begins her journey homeward]. The greater part of Harrington saw us off; not because a party of people sailing away for a distant land is unknown, for Harrington is still the [home port] of many a good vessel that take active part in the world's commerce. The fact is that visitors to Harrington are very rare, especially those who come for pleasure purely. The arrival of an automobile in town was in fact a thing that had been anticipated throughout our visit. [The travelers reach the junction of the Harrington River and the ocean.] Above us lay the long green reaches of the river and below a great black lowering wall of fog that stretched the length of the coast and the breadth of the sea, two hundred miles each way. The wind was south "in the gut of the ocean", to use Lon's expression. The iron chains thrown across the harbors of besieged medieval cities were not half so strong as this. The hand of man had made them and the hand of man might sever; but God's great bellows held the fog, and does man's whistling avail against it if the very sun itself could not dispel it? We resigned ourselves to our fate accordingly. Lon went ashore to spend the night and Tom and I turned in. [On the evening of the twentieth the fog lifted and Mermaid set sail, heading southwest, skirting Stonington, "that most uninteresting town". For the next two days it was a case of either too much or too little wind, compelling Lon to make remarks "which would hardly have pleased more sensitive ears." Hale, recalling their frustrations, waxes philosophical.]

July 24. Weather is one of mankind's greatest educators. In a calm we must be patient; in a gale we must be cool. In the calm we must be cheerful; in the gale we must have fortitude and presence of mind. Weather teaches that regulator of all virtues, temperance. But weather is unknown to the average man. He only sees what little of it that can struggle through the smoke of his factory chimneys. Rain or snow or fog are amazing things that make him take an umbrella to the office in the morning. And there the average man's knowledge of weather ceases.

Now the only real weather is on the sea where it is unmodified by outside influences. Consequently the sailor is practically the only man that knows what weather is. He is the only man on whom weather's teachings can have their effect....

Foul and fickle weather followed Mermaid and her crew on the rest of their journey. Hale's account of the remaining days and nights until they reached Cushings Island on August 4 contains little but descriptions of their determination to make it home despite their tribulations. Recalling the cruise, however, Hale expresses nothing but the self-satisfaction of someone certain that he has experienced if only briefly a life superior to all others.

One cannot know life's luxuries til he has learned its necessities.... The man who drums along the coast in his steam yacht might see as much or more scenery than we have seen. But he cannot obtain one half the pleasure. To enjoy such a trip to the full, one must live a life as radically different from the city life as the Maine scenes are different from the city scenes. He must live a life of absolute simplicity. On our whole trip Down East we did not once see a boat as small as the one we were in. Yet we three had all that could be desired and in seaworthiness and speed Mermaid proved the superior of many bigger boats.

[Another of the trip's rewards] was the acquaintance we made with so many of the people. The Maine coast has reared a class of people as unique and interesting as they are unfeignedly simple and honest, a type as foreign to the average American as the cowboy of the western plains, or even the Patagonian aborigines and South Sea cannibals. No one who has listened to the evening's conversation at the grocery store of Monhegan can doubt this. Their language is so different from the language which we ordinarily speak as to almost merit being called a dialect, and their speech is as quaint to the average listener as it is interesting to the philologist....

I can never tire of hearing the true stories of these men. There is richness of simile and metaphor and a happy choice of adjectives which are always amusing though occasionally lapsing into the profane. I have heard the stories of the trip from New York to Oporto in a... gale in which the crew had to wear rubber boots and oilskins 35 days;... of the forecastle fight between "Reub" Mitchell and the "sulky" Italian seaman;... of the capture of swordfish and shark. These are no sailor's yarns; they are the real experiences of real men and their faces bear witness to them. Such men and women as Lon and Mrs. Frye and the dozens of others of their type have given us opportunity to get outside ourselves and to find another world. And after all, should that not be the object of pleasure-seeking as much as that of Columbus. The men of [the] Maine coast towns are purely of this stock, the simplest but the most romantic, the most literal but the most poetic men of modern times. And yet these men are almost unknown to most writers to whom they would be the most picturesque of subjects....[Surprisingly, Hale appears not to have read – or even known of – Sarah Orne Jewett, who in her stories and novels was writing of just such men and women.]

Such are some of the requisites for the pleasure and education that may be derived from a trip on the glorious old coast of Maine. A Rhode Island judge has said that the knowledge of boats and boat sailings is more necessary to a man than a college education. And this I know to be true. If anyone will dispute I shall point to Lon and say: "There is a man who can barely write, who reads with difficulty and whose simple figuring is inaccurate. But he is the wisest, most honest, most lovable, noblest-hearted man I ever knew."

In 1905, Hale and Lon set out on a cruise to Gloucester. Lon took sick before they reached Cape Porpoise, however, and they were forced to turn back. The following year, accompanied by Sumner Fogg, he sailed for sixteen days to Belfast, Maine and back. Hale kept no record of that trip, remarking only in his journal that it "was far the pleasantest in history not only in itself but because it cemented a very firm friendship between myself and Sumner Fogg." (RH IV, 399-400) Reading these accounts of Hale's first two cruises, it is hard to remember that they were written when he was only sixteen. His Romantic enthusiasms may sometimes seem adolescent. But the lucidity and occasional elegance of his prose, along with his ability to observe with such care suggest an older and more experienced traveler and travel writer.

The narratives contain themes that will recur frequently in his further journals, and in the ship's logs he kept once he began to sail Thetis. He manifested a fascination with the doings and sayings of Down East men and women. He expressed as well a moralist's admiration for the spare honesty with which he saw those people living out their lives. His treasured friendship with Lon and the adventures they shared led him to believe himself part of that community of souls the two of them encountered on their journeys – a community carefully studied yet at the same time unconsciously invented. He could convince himself that he had shed the life of the summer "rusticators" he enjoyed disparaging for something less frivolous and far worthier of his time and attention. Above all, he celebrated the sea, seafaring, and the civilization it had produced Down East. The tiny country to which he pledged allegiance was bounded by the perimeter of his travels, reflected in his experiences, and grounded in his romantic imagination. Within it, he lived a very happy young man.

The Thetis Cruises, 1907-1914

With the launching of Thetis, Hale decided that his fine new boat deserved a more formal record of her life and times than he had provided Mermaid. For the next eight years he kept meticulous accounts of Thetis's annual comings and goings in and around Casco Bay, down the coast of Maine, and to and from Gloucester and Marblehead. When Thetis was sold in 1914, following the commencement of Hale's career as a young lawyer in Boston, the logs were replaced by annual accounts of "The Maritime Adventures of Robert Hale", as he continued to sail whenever he could in the waters he had come to know and love so thoroughly.

The logs were formally conceived documents, entitled each year in the same way: "Log of Sloop Thetis for the season 1907, in the year of Thetis the first, and in the year of cruises the fifth". Accompanying the title was a quotation from Kipling's ballad "The Anchor Song":

> Wheel full and by; but she'll smell her road tonight.
> Sick she is and harbour sick; O sick to clear the land.
> Roll down to Brest with the Red Ensign over us.
> Carry on and thrash her out with all she'll stand.

As those lines attest, the logs are, in addition to a record of places visited, of times and tides, a repeated declaration of Hale's love for the romance of sea and ships. They include not only accounts of annual cruises, but also of shorter trips, often with his parents, along with "the doings of the Cushings Island waterfront": day sails in Casco Bay with friends and family which, as often as not, included Hale's mother as passenger. The boat could — and often did — carry as many as eight or more on those day sails. The cruises were crewed by three or four of Hale's friends, students at Bowdoin, Dartmouth, and Harvard Law School, designated "first mate" or "able seaman" along with Hale, "captain and owner", and Lon Randall, "skipper and pilot". (See Appendix for a list and brief biographies of crew members.)

Captain Hale clearly took great pleasure in introducing this select handful to the joys he had discovered inside the world that had come to mean so much to him. Along with their captain, their tasks included writing daily entries in the logs, taken in turn. Upon the entries Hale imposed a formulaic, third-person style. Its quaintness encouraged a sense of adventuring together into territory that required a language all its own, one that further separated the sailors from their everyday lives ashore.

In addition to the daily entries, each log includes an obsessively maintained collection of charts, recording expenditures on food and sundries (for example, postal cards, soap, milk, ice cream, linament, rope, peas, gasoline, doughnuts, lobsters, soldering, etc., itemized, on pages 186 and 187 of the 1909 log); miles sailed each day of the summer aboard Thetis; daily wind direction; and wins and losses at cards by crew members.

Hale nowhere provides a detailed description of Thetis. After examining photographs, two experienced present-day sailors and boat builders, Peter Murray and Peter Plumb, both of Portland and Cushings Island, have provided useful information and conjecture that, combined with details gleaned from the logs, suggest that Thetis is best described as a stretched-out

Friendship sloop. She was probably around fifty feet in length, with another ten feet of bowsprit, equipped with mainsail, jib and flying jib, and three topsails: gaff, jib and club. The mast, approximately one foot in diameter, was constructed with a topmast that could be removed. The bow section appears to have been more substantial than that of typical pleasure yachts, suggesting that the boat's hull was patterned on contemporary fishing sloops. This makes sense, give that Lon and George Randall, both experienced commercial sailors, played a big part in her design. All in all, Thetis was, quite a boat.

Though Thetis was not herself equipped with a gas engine, the launch Achilles was, and often towed the larger boat out of harbor and into the wind. (Recall Achilles was Thetis's son.) The stove, used for both cooking and heating, was fueled by coal and wood, which came aboard, along with other provisions, at the start of each cruise, replenished when necessary during the trip. In a typical entry, written the day before the commencement of the 1909 cruise, Hale records: "The crew work hard on Thetis stowing away wood and coal and doing odd jobs without number. Also [an important essential] get aboard library, and other last minute comforts" (RH VIII, 39). Those comforts included one or more bottles of rum – "grog" in the language of the log – which was drunk in moderation on many evenings and on celebratory occasions.

If the captain and his crew drank moderately, they ate heartily. Part of most meals came from cans, loaded aboard at the start of the trip. But the crew supplemented that standard fare with delicacies from local markets: beef steak, haddock, "corned hake", lobster, blueberries, ice cream – "the rich congealed foam of browsing kine, as Shakespeare so well puts it". (RH VIII, 140). Lon, who did most of the cooking, produced griddle cakes, buckwheat cakes, and johnny cakes. To greet Fulton Redman, "first mate and engineer" on his belated arrival aboard Thetis in 1911, his fellow sailors spread a feast. As reported by Hale: "All hands sit down to one of the most elaborate meals ever served since the famous Lucullus first tickled his palate with the juicy ortolan. Beef, corn, onions, potatoes, cranberry, pies, cake, fruit, and candy composed a repast which guaranteed complete inertia for the remainder of the day." (RH XI, 39). Though others took a hand in the galley occasionally, it was Lon they relied upon for their steady carbohydrate-heavy diet. Once when a cold laid Lon low and "able seaman" A.T. Gould took his place at the stove, the latter recorded that "all hands remained more or less hungry for the rest of the day". (RH XII, 42) And when sailing in rough weather or at odd times of day or night the fare was often little more than rice or beans and applesauce. (Hale once complained that "applesauce was more than a mere feature" one evening.) (RH XI, 24).

Readying Thetis for the season required considerable hard work, most of which fell to Lon and one or two other local boat builders. Arriving to inspect work in progress in early May of 1909, Hale "finds A. Randall planing down the main boom." Though he hopes the boat will be "in better shape than ever" within a month, those hopes are dashed by a spate of bad weather. On Memorial Day, Hale reports that Thetis "has never been in such rough condition at this the opening of the season. Decks are untouched, although her spars are in A1 condition and davits, etc., have been fixed. And if the fine weather of this day is any augury of good, the season of 1909 will indeed be the greatest ever. Such, at any rate, is the fond hope of Thetis's crew who look to see her this year handsomer as well as stiffer than ever before." (RH VIII, 1, 3, 7-8)

Once aboard and asail, the crew worked hard to keep Thetis handsome and stiff, scraping, painting, polishing brass. On the 1908 cruise, while moored at Marblehead: "The crew arrive early to take advantage of the excellent day for painting. All hands turn to and sandpaper, scrape, and work all day, taking a short time to eat dinner." The following year they were at it once more. With Hale and Lon in town buying provisions, the rest of the crew "turn to on the paint work". On his return from town Lon "delights all hands with a splendid fish chowder of which the greater part is gobbled up in a few minutes. This encouraged the mates to start to work on the paint work again; and…they completed the painting of bulwarks and sides, and varnishing of decks and cockpit until Thetis was resplendent.…" (RH VII, 88; VIII, 113)

When repair rather than maintenance was the issue, Lon could often attend successfully to the matter at hand. On the 1911 cruise the head, "Aunt Nellie", erupted. "Especially worthy of remark among things antecedent to gaining anchorage is an incident which caused no small vexation to Lon. 'Someone had blundered' in his use of the apparatus aboard for meeting the needs of nature. Oversight and failure to adjust a lever gave entrance to the sea, part of which Lon noticed washing about the cabin. He knew the cause of such a phenomenon, possibly by instinct, and set all right in no time, but not without words, incriminations and a dustpan and bucket." (RH XI, 26) The following year, "Aunt Nellie" erupted again. This time, the fault lay with her innards. "In response to Aunt Nellie's constant demands for attention, [two crew members] went ashore and secured the services of a Gloucester specialist who prescribed what appeared to be a proper remedy and exacted what appeared to be an improper fee." (RH XII, 37).

Assuaging the needs of the launch Achilles was a frequent chore. A few days before the Aunt Nellie crisis of 1912, an electrician was brought aboard to rewire the engine "which refuses to stop unless disconnected". (RH XII, 27) More often the engine refused to start. On one such occasion, the crew placed itself in the hands of the Almighty.

It is happily suggested that there may be some virtue in naming the books of the Bible, and as it was the Sabbath such an exercise seemed not wholly unbecoming. Accordingly "Genesis, Exodus, Leviticus, Deuteronomy, I Numbers, II Numbers, I Kings, II Kings, Samuel, Epistle to the Ephesians". Then a vigorous turn to the flywheel. Nothing doing. Collosians and Galatians were tried without avail. But at the magic name of Timothy she started—backwards. Thus does our Sunday School training help us in time of great need. (RH XII, 16-17)

That entry, written by perennial crew member Albert Gould, reflects the spirit of gentle foolishness that prevailed aboard Thetis. The sailors used the log to poke fun at their fellows. Everyday activities evoked mock debates: herring vs. sardines, "the subject of many heated disputes and an opportunity to hear what law school can do for a man"; or salt water vs. fresh water bathing, which the more hygienic? (RH VIII, 74, 76; XII, 15)

During the day, when not sailing or laboring to keep Thetis shipshape, crew members swam – though Captain Hale abstained, self-conscious perhaps of his lack of form. Usually at least once during a cruise, "to serve lagging appetites", the men competed against each other by rowing in sprints from Thetis to a nearby mooring. And when at Marblehead they sometimes entered Thetis in yacht club races. In 1912 they finished second of four in their class the first day. On the second, they came close to colliding with another sloop, Clorinda.

When about one mile from Mark 4 we are on starboard tack close hauled [and therefore have the right-of-way] and a sloop bears down on us on the port tack. Expecting her…to tack we continued on our course but to our amazement Clorinda kept on across our bow. Capt. Hale luffed sharp in order to avoid staving a hole in Clorinda's side and in so doing saved the sloop from sinking. As it was, her rigging fouled on our bowsprit and her mast came down on deck. [There was concern for one of the Clorinda's crew.] We were told [he] was not seriously hurt for which we were sincerely glad even though we know that no blame rests on us…. [RH XII, 33-35]

This account serves as reminder that captain and crew of Thetis were where they were, doing what they did, because they loved to sail. Whether or not all of the crew were as accomplished sailors as Hale, they appear to have been at least familiar with the rudiments of navigation and the craft of seamanship. In the case of Fulton Redman, Hale's most dedicated fellow traveler, his experience of boats and boating did equal that of his captain. One of Albert Gould's log entries makes the point eloquently, as he describes their approach to the harbor at Blue Hill during the 1909 cruise.

At 8:05[a.m.] entered Bartlett's Narrows, the most beautiful inside sailing we have seen yet…. Tide was setting out of bay; R. Hale takes the wheel, F.J. Redman lends his assistance as pilot, J.L. Crosby stands by fore-topsail, and A.T. Gould immolates himself on end of bowsprit on lookout for shallow water. From this unprejudiced standpoint he can safely aver, as he now does in truth, that the way R. Hale and F.J. Redman took the good ship into Blue Hill Harbor was as neat and skillful a piece of seamanship as anybody would ask to see. With scarcely room to work in, they beat past the rocks at the mouth of the harbor, worked over to the ledges near Steamboat Wharf, just missed running down red buoy, and shot up for an anchorage in the best spot in the harbor. (RH VIII, 53-54)

During the 1911 cruise, in an evening storm, Thetis, moored in North East Harbor, began to drag both her anchors.

Sea choppy, Thetis jumping around and wind still blowing what A. Randall and R. Hale [who is writing the log entry] took to be the hardest of their nine summers of cruising. Get down on top of unknown steam yacht of about our own size [anchored nearby]. All hands stand by with oars and fenders to keep her clear. Two hours hard work while the wind keeps on and the barometer falls to 29.68. Thetis all the time dragging slowly. About 7 bells all hands stand by to give out all remaining chain with a corresponding amount of hauser on the big anchor, and to fend the steamer off bowsprit if possible. Accomplish the result without much damage to either boat as far as could be judged. As R. Hale sang out "8 bells" all hands were forward watching chain and Thetis was lying more easily with 60 fathoms…out on her two anchors. (RH XI, 35)

Close encounters of that kind were the exception. Far more often, there would be a glorious day such as Hale, Lon, and friend John Crosby experienced during a short, late-season cruise in 1909.

Off Sugar Loaves all hands gather for'ard for impromptu meal. Breezes up here, and start a little sheet. A. Randall gives the word "WSW and let her ball". And let her ball we did. Out in West Penobscot Bay the wind was blowing fresh and heavy, like a fall breeze, and the sea worked up quite a bit of chop. Every few minutes, a fountain of spray leapt up from [Thetis's] weather bow and fell all over the good ship in showers, till even the faces of the crew in the cockpit were heavily encrusted with salt and the spindrift whirled away from her lee in a feather-white smother of foam. It was wonderful sailing, and the crew voted it the very best of the season. (RH VIII, 139)

As much as sailing like that lay at the heart of the weeks aboard Thetis, its captain and crew were frequently compelled to spend their days and nights fogbound. They did their best to endure the tedium, Hale perhaps recalling his philosophical remarks written back in 1906 about the resignation required to endure those times when "God's great bellows holds the fog, and man, despite his whistling, cannot prevail against them." On Thetis's maiden voyage the following year, the sailors rose on the morning of July 15 to find that "the fates had turned against us and buried us deep in fog as thick as burgoo." At first they attempted to appease Aeolus, mythical keeper of the winds, with ritual: "There we stood attired in white duck uniform with bended head and hat across our breasts while begging Aeolus for propitious winds for our journey to Gloucester." Aeolus paid his supplicants no attention. The following day, they tried a song:

> Somewhere a little sunshine,
>
> Somewhere a little rain.
>
> Fog is thicker 'an burgoo
>
> Down in Jonesport, Maine.

By evening, with no sign of a change, they concluded that the fault lay with Mate Sumner Fogg: "This is Fogg's birthday. All the fogs for miles around have blown into Jonesport to help make Sumner enjoy the day."

On the seventeenth: "Mate Fogg's birthday has taken on the appearance of a protracted spree, for still all the fogs are with us....The natives hold various opinions....Some say it will clear in a day; others that it will last at least a month. It is hard to believe one, but harder still to doubt the other." Not until July 19 are they able to escape —only to find themselves immediately becalmed. (RH VI, 40 ff.)

At times such as that the sailors became acutely conscious of the fact that a cruise was about the seacoast as well as the sea. Bad weather dictated days spent ashore. Here is Gould describing an excursion to Bar Harbor by steamer from Winter Harbor, where fog had becalmed the crew for nearly a week in 1911.

There being no hope of a clear-off [we] went ashore to try to forget that we had been swinging around over our potato peelings for nearly a week.... Mr. Redman donned his frock coat, stuck a pink in his button hole and marched up the bank humming "Casey Jones". [They boarded S.S. Schoodic for Bar Harbor] where we strolled along the main thoroughfares, and then along the famous Shore Path. From the path we had a fine view of the summer cottages that face the sea and are backed by the hills. Mr. Redman here selected a spot for his future castle. (RH XI, 42-43)

Trips for provisions frequently combined encounters with both past and present. On that same cruise, they went ashore at Port Clyde in search of fresh milk.

On the way we boarded the old "New Boxer", an aged old coaster built in 1845 now going to ruin, and fated to spend her last days as a gasoline hulk. With…charts stored in the cabin she seemed to be waiting to go on a last voyage on the sea of death. After sitting awhile in the shadow of her windlass and listening to her disconsolate creaking against the wharf, we tramped down the road to Marshall's Point….where we waited for the "women folks" to return, and listened to Mr. Marshall's account of the good old days of clipper ships and Yankee crews. At last with a full pail of milk we found our way back to Thetis – and turned in, to be rocked to sleep by the groundswell. (RH XI, 24-25)

Two years earlier, while again in search of milk, this time at Jonesport, they found the stores "all short up," the day being Sunday;

so we went along from house to house in search of milk, while a little child led us, our mate [John Crosby] having captivated him. Then we strolled down to the waterfront and inspected Jim Beal's lobster boat, which was up for sale. Milford Beal, "uncle Ben's boy," joined us and pointed out the reach-boat he owned, of which he was more proud than Lucifer; inspected the "Always Ready" which does a freight business between Jonesport and neighboring ports; and then fell in with the corpulent skipper of the "Eva Race" who was in search of men to go herring fishing. (RH VIII, 62-63)

The visitors on more than this occasion attracted the attention of children, no doubt because they marked the crew as fair game. Hale reports in 1908 that Gould "undertakes a becoming charity by giving some children peppermint candy, but thereby gets himself into difficulties altogether unexpected. These are solved only by purchase and delivery of further candies to the injured parties". (RH XI, 39)

The following year, while in Jonesport seeing to the repair

of a galvanized iron gas tank, Hale and Crosby encounter the repairman's son Levi, aged 11 and "the best left fielder in Jonesport. Levi returns with us and 'doesn't care' if he has a little ham and eggs...." A little of Levi apparently went a long way, for when the crew returned to Jonesport several days later, Hale and Gould on a "walk to the westward", struggled through a marsh on the way back to avoid him, after his threats "to fetch them when they came back." (RH VIII, 65, 75)

The logs' authors take pleasure in their encounters with local "characters": the Congregational minister at Jonesport in 1911, preacher of so "powerful" a sermon that it could be heard a block away from the church; "a thin gentleman" at Winter Harbor that same year "who said he was 'the feller that enforces the law', and hereupon displayed a Deputy Sheriff's badge. He, at the same time informed us that he is going to vote 'wet' on September 11". (RH XI, 51, 37)

In one important respect the Thetis logs differ from the accounts Hale wrote when sailing with Lon aboard Mermaid. Now when the crew goes ashore it is as often as not to enjoy the company of college contemporaries and their female counterparts. Especially when Thetis pointed her bow westward, cruising for a week or more to Gloucester and Marblehead, where Hale's grandmother and aunt lived during the summer, time spent ashore meant time with the sort of ladies and gents whom Hale had disparaged as "rusticators" when he was younger. In the process, sex – decorous, well-chaperoned sex, to be sure – began to rear its head.

Social life at Marblehead centered on the Hawthorne Inn, to which the crew was wont to go of an evening. In August of 1909, following dinner as guests of a friend of Hale's aunt, the crew "meet two ladies with whom the mates of Thetis are well-pleased. Chat on the piazza until 10pm". When Hale and Redman suggest that it's time to call it a night, "they were captured by the two cherubic young ladies and it was with difficulty that the mates dragged the two other members of the crew away at 11 o'clock". (RH VIII, 103-104). Still in Marblehead several days later, Hale records his companions' thoughts on East Coast high living.

We sit on deck fascinated as we have always been with the effervescence of life in the pleasure-laden waters of Marblehead. Here it seems to us is not the Roman luxury that saps the young energy of rich and weakens the heart of the nation [as at Bar Harbor, presumably], but honest healthy pleasure, which is wholesome if it be expensive, and honorable though it may be ultra-fashionable. At all event the glamor of harbor lights and the music of the band with the heavens lit irregularly by flashes of lightning from clouds banked to leeward – all this wrought its inevitable effect upon our minds. (RH VIII, 111)

The limits of "honest healthy pleasure" were perhaps tested three years later at the Inn, when, as recorded by Gould, "two attractive ladies fresh from the New York stage demonstrated how the Turkey Trot should be danced, while the admiring youths of the hotel applauded." Yet, "by 11 o'clock we were again out under the clear stars rowing off to Thetis, each of us thinking of the good bunks awaiting us." (RH XII, 39)

Despite their enthusiasm for the attractions of the Hawthorne Inn, the crew remained more than content with evenings spent aboard Thetis. Before retiring to their good bunks they almost always indulged in one or more rounds of a Canadian card game called 63. Popular in New Brunswick and Nova Scotia and featuring lively bidding wars, it bears resemblance to euchre. A maximum bid is sixty-three; hence the name. Every cruise included fierce rivalries between two teams, sometimes "Champions" v. "Would-Bes", sometimes Bowdoin v. Harvard.

Results of all matches are recorded at the end of each log book; contests are described with various degrees of heavy-handed jollity. Here is Hale in 1908, on a triumph by the "Would-Bes". "Two more games of sixty-three bring more laurels to the Would-Bes and especially to Mate Fogg. Mate Fogg played a game of scintillating brilliancy, placing his cards with all his native shrewdness and making his bids with a daring but infallible judgment. Indeed we safely predict that when this youth comes to years of discretion and understanding, he will astonish the world by his executive ability, as much as he now dazzles it with his social triumphs." (RH VII, 68)

When not debauching at cards, the crew read, and with discrimination. Gould is recorded as engrossed in Balzac's *Pere Goriot* on the 1909 cruise; Hale, in his journal, lists his readings "extra curriculum" from 1911 to 1915. They include several works by H. G. Wells and J. K. Chesterton, Hardy's *Tess*, and Wilde's *De Profundis.* Nonetheless many an evening was spent in little more than what Hale described once as "diligent idleness" (RH VIII, 95). Sometimes that meant speculating about a future far from a life in the law. One evening in 1909, following a stroll through the streets of Jonesport, where "many of the people we met recognized R. Hale and F. Redman, and we soon felt ourselves to be in the bosom of our friends", the mates returned to Thetis and found themselves asking what each of them would do "in case the fields in which they have chosen to labor should not [produce a harvest] after the first few tickles of the hoe; and by acclamation it was voted to come to Jonesport and go herring fishing." (RH VIII, 64) Two years later, while at Brooklin, Hale rhapsodized about a farmhouse he had spotted while on a stroll ashore "as a future abode for himself when he gives up the idea of becoming 'learned' and seeks solace in farming and fishing." (RH XI, 30)

On other nights "idle diligence" took the form of telling and retelling yarns about sea and seacoast – in the process imbibing the romance of a past close by the present that lay before them every day. On the 1913 cruise, Hale records Fulton Redman piloting Thetis to harbor in Berry's Cove, near Lamoine, where Redman had spent summers as a boy.

He regaled his shipmates with a profusion of anecdotes…and stories of the four-masters that used to load ice from Blunt's Pond and coasters that used to go down through the narrows…. After dinner on deck, as the sun set in a cold, yellow sky, there were memories and portraits of bygone men and days. The evening ended with all hands… telling tales of coasters that would sail and coasters that wouldn't. The night was cold and magnificently starlit, with still a little nor'west air. The harbor seemed a great beautiful pond. (RH XIII, 34-35)

No doubt Lon took part in the telling of those tales, repeating the stories he had poured out to Hale on their first Mermaid cruise: "passages to the Indies, to Oporto or the perils of the coaster". At times he would join in with the collegiate hi-jinks going on around him. On the 1909 cruise, he served as judge during the "famous trial" at which Redman and Gould stood accused as "soreheads on the question of Hawthorne Inn girls," the defendants having disparaged a couple of the inn's recent young lady guests.

Mr. Gould and Mr. Redman appeared as their own advocates, but Mr. Hale and Mr. Crosby showed conclusively the weakness of the Harvard men's position. However, Judge Randall asked for three weeks in which to sum up the case. For a time voices rang high in Thetis' cabin, and glasses jumped crazily from the table. Peace finally spread her wings, Redman heading bunkward at 8p.m., closely followed by Gould (worn out with further argument), and later by the others. (RH VIII, 108)

Lon played along willingly enough with these shenanigans.

Yet reading the logs, one can't escape the sense that for much of the time he remained a shadowy figure, part seasoned mentor, part obliging upper servant; proffering expert advice one minute, serving up chowder and johnny cakes the next. When the crew goes ashore he almost always remains behind, especially while they lie at anchor in Marblehead. He is certainly no longer perceived as central to the story, as he was when sailing with Hale aboard Mermaid.

Yet he unquestionably remained central to Hale's summers and to his life. If proof were needed, it lies in a moving passage from Hale's Oxford journal written in March 1913 upon learning from his mother that Lon had suffered a stroke.

Heaven knows if he will live. I lay on the couch and wept the first tears that have come in my eyes for a long time; and even now I can't bear to think calmly. He has been the instructor, guide and inspiration of all my best life. Beside my mother, I don't believe any human has influenced me so much and so finely. I can see his bearded, sad face on the pillow and [hear] the thick "Robert, Sonnie" with which he would greet me if I could see him. When he was well and aboard the boat, it was "morning Cap'n" shouted very gaily that first met my ears. I would do anything to feel his huge hand with the yellow fever marks. But there is nothing I can do but write him, and death may have paralyzed him utterly before this slow letter reaches.

O the pity of life that I cannot express, cannot make him know the love I have for him. Every memory of the last ten years of sailing is a thought of him…. It was from him I learned all my useful knowledge, the only knowledge I am not ashamed of. It was with him I shared all the best of my experience, looking always to that sad, old face for counsel and advice, and never failing to find it in all its wealth. Age never stood between us, nor education. I know two men were never more soul to soul than we. I had a premonition in September I had said my last goodbye to him. Pray God I was wrong and may clasp his hand again. (RH XVI, 174-175)

Hale's prayer was answered. When he returned to Maine in

the summer, he once more clasped that hand in his; by August, Lon was capable of short day sails. Though he lived on for several more years, however, he never again cruised as he had on those happy early excursions.

Thus Thetis and her crews, as they sailed together from Jonesport to Marblehead in the summers from 1907 to 1914. What follow are fuller excerpts from the log of the cruise of 1910. Read now, the repetitions and details contained in the day-after-day entries can grow monotonous. But, in a sense, that is their point. Hale and his mates, without perhaps realizing it, used the logs to shape the minutia of their lives together into a set of rituals that became the fabric of the world they were creating, its rhythms and – ultimately – its permanence as memory. The log of 1910 is, perhaps, the best exemplar of that process. It contains some of the liveliest writing within the 1,434 pages that comprise the history of "good ship" Thetis, her captain, her skipper, and her mates.

Illustrations

All photos, unless otherwise credited, are from the Thetis Logs. The captions in quotations are by Hale.

Thetis, 1907

Log

of

SLOOP THETIS

FOR THE SEASON

of

A.D. 1910

Cras in gens iterabimus aequor.
Αἰὲν ἀριστεύειν καὶ ὑπείροχον ἔμμεναι ἄλλων

IN THE YEAR OF THE THETIS, THE FOURTH, AND IN THE YEAR OF CRUISES, THE EIGHTH.

CUSHING'S ISLAND COVE.

Robert Hale	Captain and Owner
Alonzo Randall	Skipper and Pilot
~~Fulton Jarvis~~ Redman.	First Mate and Engineer
Albert Trowbridge Gould	
John Leland Crosby.	Able Seamen
Thomas Albert Foster.	
Robert Dillingham Morse.	

Also a brief account of the doings of the Cushing's Island Waterfront

First page of the 1910 log. The quotations are from Virgil
and Homer: "Tomorrow we will venture on to the sea";
"Always to excel and continue to surpass others".

Port Clyde Harbor, ca. 1900. (Courtesy of
Marshall Point Lighthouse Museum)

Eastern Yacht Club, Marblehead. (Courtesy of Eastern Yacht Club)

Thetis, "A bone in her mouth". 1909

Thetis, "By the wind off Provincetown". 1908

"Lon Randall at the wheel". 1907

Randall: "With eyes that look backwards into the years". 1909

Margaret Hale aboard Thetis. 1908

Lon Randall, Fulton Redman, Albert Gould,
John Crosby, aboard Thetis. 1909

Fulton Redman. 1908

Fulton Redman, "A modern Hercules." 1909

Captain Hale on a day sail, with two "fair maidens". 1908

The Cruise of 1910

Hale paid his first visit of the season to Thetis on April 16, just two months shy of his graduation from Bowdoin.

> For the first time since September 19, 1909, R. Hale sets foot aboard the good ship. She is rolling heavily in the undertow of Whitehead Channel. At work upon her are A. Randall and Allen Fisher. They have been able to do excellent work considering the season. All the spars have been scraped and varnished and the starboard side scraped clean of paint. Everything alow and aloft has wintered well. And the prospects for the season were never more encouraging. (RH, IX, 1-2)

Once free from his college obligations, Hale spent every day on the water. By July 4 the crew had assembled; in addition to Hale and Lon: Fulton Redman, Albert Gould, John Crosby, and Thomas Foster, by now all seasoned veterans. A final loading of supplies, followed by the customary visit to "The Ottawa House tonsorial parlor", and they are off. (All subsequent excerpts from RH IX, 30ff).

> [July 8. By Hale]… At 9:42, R. Hale hoists the new private signal to the masthead and the cruise is officially begun….Up anchor at 1:45 and run down [Great] Diamond Island thoroughfare at the rate of about 1½ knots…. R. Hale records the bets of the crew on the first appearance of [Lon's] famous story about Kettle Island [apparently a perennial favorite], the pool to consist of ice creams. Then followed a brilliant succession of anecdotes told by all the members of the crew. In this department T. A. Foster developed remarkable propensities as a raconteur. [They anchor in Pott's Harbor at 5:30.] Supper and then all but A. Randall ashore. Buy postals, etc. Secure the competent services of Mr. Wallace to get [Achilles'] engine wired up. Return at nine to read books and converse. Perfectly calm as usual. Glass at 29.98. Redman does some shadowboxing on deck. Turn in at ten o'clock.

> [July 9. By Gould] Our slumbers were somewhat troubled by Redman's night-before threat to pipe all hands on deck at 3 a.m. We "fell for that

noise" but nothing came of it. The stilly night silence was unbroken until A. Randall rattled the dishes at seven o'clock…. "Social amenities" compel Redman's attendance at a dance in nearby Bath. [The remainder of the crew set sail mid-morning, only to be foiled by a lack of wind.] At 11:45a.m. dropped the palm of the anchor into the harbor from which it had been reluctantly dragged an hour and 36 minutes before….

After dinner all hands went ashore to have the engine repaired and also to partake of ice cream and checkerberry "lossengers". After a general debauch in the ice cream parlor and a stroll up the road to the blacksmith shop, all hands visited the Harpswell Yacht Club float where Capt. Hale gave evidence, by turning all the valves on the engine, that he had reached the last stages of the motorboat disease of tinkeritis.

On board Thetis Crosby indulged in unlimited conversation and a very limited swim, while Foster, with what he called periwinkles for bait, thought he could beguile the artless flounders into impaling themselves on the rusty hook he lowered to the muddy bottom. Potetters and onions were soon steaming on the table. They steamed for only a few minutes, and then were gone; and Crosby fell back on the locker and slumbered heavily….

[July 10. By Redman] Breakfast at 7:30 after Gould, Crosby and Redman had taken their morning plunge. The day does not look particularly good for sailing but we get underway at 9:22…. Use launch for a few minutes to stem the tide off Haddock Rock…. Hold good breeze S by W and round Cuckolds at 12:10. Wind flushes out. Decide to put in to Boothbay.

[July 11. By Crosby] Hoping to reach Belfast we are underway at the early hour of 7:25…. Blew from the land a scorching breeze. Off Spruce Head at 4:45, at which point Capt. Hale relinquished the wheel after one of the best tricks at wheel he ever had. Breeze slacked considerably, but puffs out of Belfast Bay brought us into an anchorage off Belfast Fuel and Hay Wharf at 6:45.

Foster goes ashore to prepare Belfast for our coming, and with supper and toilet completed it is about 8:30 when we land…. We spend a pleasant evening on the piazza of the Quimby mansion [friends of Foster]…. In honor of a run of 54 miles, the first rations of grog were served on our return to Thetis, and at about 11:30 on a perfectly calm and starlit night, Thetis' bunks were once more full.

[July 12. By Foster] The crew, after their dip into Belfast social circles, anticipated a long "beauty sleep" on this morning. But A. Randall and F. Redman, unable to sleep on account of troubled minds, "noise around" and cause other more sensible members to crawl out at 6. Light breeze NW. Glass 30.8. Prospects of an attractive and saucy day. Breakfast at 6:30.... [The crew spends the morning making social calls in Belfast.]

All hands on Thetis at 11. At 11:20 under jib sails along on her way eastward.... F. Redman prepares excellent dinner after which T. Foster and A. Gould fall into deep and blessed sleep. [They head for Brooklin Harbor], R. Hale at the wheel. F. Redman on the bow had to keep Capt. Hale posted on the harbor ledges. Dropped anchor at 4:35. F. Redman hustles ashore, ostensibly for milk.

After an hour he returns with only 3 quarts of the beverage.... R. Hale becomes enthusiastic about rowing races. A. Gould and R. Hale compete over a 100 yd. course. No doubt victory would have perched aboard the bow of R. Hale's skiff had he not unlocked port oar.... At 5:30 all hands gather at table to attack a bushel of meal gruel. Crosby makes record. Crosby and Foster go ashore without getting into any trouble. The harbor is filled with the shrill voices of feminine picnickers. This disturbance does not cease until 10:15. R. Hale and T. Foster recover old strength and decisively defeat A. Gould and F. Redman at 63. Gould goes ashore with mail; after his return all hands turn in, having been served with grog in dainty fashion by Crosby. Night calm, moon partly covered with wisp of cloud.

[July 13. By Hale. Fog drives Thetis into Bass Harbor by mid-morning.] A fisherman rowing by in a peapod remarks to us, with the assuring manner of the Delphic priestess, "She'll lay there all night." The crew decided his meaning to be (a) that Thetis had a good berth and would not go adrift; (b) that the weather would be such that Thetis could not get away for a long period; (c) that Thetis had a bad berth and would be stuck in the flats when we opted to go out. Optimism favors (a). [Rain compels the crew to turn to "literary pursuits" and 63.]

[July 14. By Redman.] Fine clear morning with no wind.... After breakfast the Captain of the Edissa [a sloop anchored nearby] came aboard and attempted to start the launch. After working hard for more than an hour he was obliged to give up his attempt, remarking that this was the first time he was ever beaten by an engine. [They depart for North East Harbor.] Drop anchor at 12:05. All hands except Skipper Randall go ashore in afternoon for mail, ice cream, ship stores, etc. J. Crosby and F. Redman have a swim before supper. After supper the crew seek amusement and pleasure in various places.... All hands are turned in at midnight.

[July 15. By Gould.] A feeling of fog in the air did not deter our hardy captain from getting ready for a run across the bay. The drowsy revelers of last night were dragged on deck, treated to the rope's end by A. Randall, and sent forward to heave her short. Second Mate [Gould] tried the harbor water and found it had a down-east tang and bite. After fine breakfast of ham and eggs, with bananas to top off on, sail was made and the anchor came aboard at 7:12a.m. [They sail to South West Harbor in search of Mayo's shop, where they have been assured they will find a cure for Achilles' ailing engine.] Mr. Mayo took charge of the launch; and guaranteed to have her in running order by the time Thetis returned from Jonesport. We felt more confidence in entrusting launch to Mr. Mayo, as his intelligence about motorboats was manifestly superior to that of the friends at Bass Harbor.... [They sail on to Jonesport, by way of the Mt. Desert shore, where – one can surmise from what follows – Redman had come a-calling two days before.] We slipped along by North East and Seal Harbor, while Mate Redman sat sorrowfully... and watched the great hills shouldering the sky and marching boldly to the north, rank after rank, like giants of old, and the coast slipping by.... R. Hale stretched her out for Schoodic, and "a lashed it to her".

[Following a dinner of lobster stew they sail on to Jonesport. Upon arrival] each man was stationed at his post, and at the command of Capt. Hale, all head sails were to drop at once; but when the command came the jib-topsail downhaul fouled, and jib halyard fouled, so the sails came down in some disorder. Capt. Dunbar of schooner Eva A. Race volunteered loud, profane and unnecessary information as to a good berth.... All hands wrote letters, while A. Randall advised us merely "to let her know we were living." At 8:15 went ashore; post office closed;... had a so-called ice cream in a shop where a fat barber plied his trade on one side of the room, while he smoked a "twofer" and hummed a popular song of ten years ago. On the other side of the room the barber's fat son vended sodas and candy; and giggled. Crosby and Redman afterwards did some shadowboxing on the dock. Returned to Thetis and had grog. All turned in as the church clock struck ten; all loaded down with peanuts, candy, ice cream and grog.

[July 16. By Crosby.] Typical Jonesport weather greets the crew as they arise for breakfast: rainy with a light southerly breeze. A cry for 63 is soon heard and Bowdoin [Hale and Crosby] throws herself into the breach, but loses to Harvard Law [Gould and Redman], 507 to 319. Although the skipper threatened to knock with the sump handle any man who attempted to refill the syrup jar, the feat was successfully performed by Redman. This in honor of a pile of matchless flapjacks, each of which measured a full 9 inches in diameter....

[July 17. By Foster. The crew engages Dan Sawyer of Jonesport and his launch for a day's excursion to Head Harbor.] Capt. Sawyer knew every rock, and took us near enough to speak to them all. Once in the circle of these waters one feels an atmosphere of the old ages in the air. It requires effort to realize that the people who make their living in these waters are citizens of the United States. Ledges and weirs are on all hands. A stranger would feel helpless in these surroundings. Captain Dan with calm assurance held his one tiller rope and "slewed" the Emeline safely through the ledges. Every turn presented a picture.

At last Head Harbor came into view; two wharves jutted into the sea indicating that many thousands of fish had been handled on this bleak, gaunt island. Only five dwelling houses stood on the head and of these only two had ever felt a covering of paint. Surely no part of the Maine coast appears more primitive. [They anchor in Pilot Cove and go ashore to scale "the Thetis mountains".] From these peaks a flood of impressions overwhelmed us all. Robert Louis Stevenson could have written a story more beautiful than *Kidnapped* and more mysterious than *Treasure Island*.... Here it was that the English pirates came to anchor in their pilot boats, rowed ashore, climbed the head and looked to the west for vessels bound into the Bay of Fundy.... Those were the days when sailing masters were our greatest men, and shipping was at its height.... [In the evening, following their return] Curtis Mansfield came aboard and told us about "herrin' vessels".... Grog was served, and all turned in but R. Hale and T. Foster…. The moon has grown larger and seems proud to pour his golden treasure upon the quiet blue waters.

[July 18. By Hale.]

> 'Tis said the swan doth sing before he dies;
> 'Twere better others died before they sung.
> But Bos'n Crosby sings before he wakes
> And then his shipmates wish that he were hung.

This pithy epigram with the suggestive analogy of Crosby and the swan explains why the crew arose more eagerly at the bos'n's instigation than they did at the mate's outcry this cold morning. All hands came on deck at 3:30 to find a clear morning with an air NE. Glass at 30.10. At 3:55 our anchor leaves its well worn hole in the Jonesport mud and Thetis fills away…. The forenoon is marked by some very notable events in the forensic line. The principals in contests were Gould, negative, and Foster, affirmative, on the question of declaration of all taxable property; Redman, affirmative, and Hale, negative, on setting clock ahead three hours in summer in order to bring about earlier rising [a topic inspired, no doubt, by their own very early rising that morning. At South West Harbor they fetch the repaired Achilles, "running in a most satisfactory way"; then on to North East Harbor, where they drop anchor at 3:55p.m.] After supper mate Redman goes off again to Seal Harbor to make a further study of the seals which disport so numerously in those waters.

[July 19. By Redman.] This day breaks with a wet looking sky…. All hands sit down to one of Skipper Randall's excellent ham and egg breakfasts. [Following a game of 63, Redman departs yet again for Seal Harbor; Foster and Crosby take the steamer for Bar Harbor, the rest remain aboard to sand and varnish the decks. Redman returns in time to sit down to "a bountiful supper".] At 9:45 Mr. Foster and Mr. Crosby come aboard with glowing accounts of their trip to Bar Harbor. On reaching [the town] they planned to buy a half dozen bananas and a glass of soda for luncheon but they were immediately taken in tow by hospitable friends, were dined, taken out driving, presented with cigars and introduced to million heirs [sic]. Mr. Henry Teague, Dartmouth, 1901, was the host and proved a royal entertainer. They were shown the Italian garden of the Kennedy estate [Kenarden, one of Bar Harbor's grandest "cottages"] by special permission of the owners. They boarded the boat for humble, quiet

North East Harbor at 7 o'clock, tired from the social turmoil of the day but still chock full of enthusiasm.

[Wednesday, July 20. By Gould. The crew once again go ashore and then in two directions. Hale and Redman spend a largely uneventful day in and around Ellsworth. Gould, Foster, and Crosby, meanwhile, attend an unanticipated picnic.] Shortly after R. Hale and F. J. Redman had departed for Ellsworth, Mr. Henry Teague's twin-screw motorboat came up the harbor, and Mr. Teague's voice was heard from afar, shouting "want to go on a picnic?" We assented with alacrity; and were soon spinning towards So[uth] West H[arbo]r, where picnic baskets and picnickers were lined up on the float. We went ashore and met many fair women and brave men. Soon we were on our way, in four launches, to Baker's Island. There was a fresh easterly blowing, and off Little Cranberry Island we all shipped some water; but arrived wet and happy at Baker's Is. at noon. A path led over the island to the S.E. side; and we followed where it led over a grassy slope, underneath the white lighthouse, through thick spruces where the air was warm and heavy with balsam, and down to flat ledges at the base of which the waves rolled in and broke in splintering showers of foam which were shot through by the sun. There on the rocks we built our fire, cooked the lobsters and boiled the coffee. After a hearty repast, the party divided itself into convenient groups; and spent the afternoon pleasantly until it was time to return to So. West Harbor. The sea was now smooth; and the run back was uneventful.

Mr. Teague, who was the moving spirit of the day, insisted on our staying to dinner. At his house we met Mr. Teague's mother and sister, and had spring chicken and many other delicacies. After dinner we walked to the Stanley house and there watched the sunset deepen over the Mt. Desert Hills. There was a moving picture show in the "big tent", and we packed in there, and saw "Peary at the Pole" and "Roosevelt's Africa". After the "show", Capt. Clark Hopkins, storm-scarred veteran of a hundred gales, spun yarns for us about his experiences at sea, ...of his being cast away in a barrel, and being later washed up on the beach of a strange island. The lights of the Ocean House were shining brightly, and Mr. Teague proposed a dance. At the dance, T. Foster distinguished himself by his rendition of the Spanish Dance. Near midnight the dance broke up after J. Crosby had played Home Sweet Home; though the playing of the bos'n and the termination of the dance had no causal relation with each other. Mr. Teague brought us home to Thetis in his launch. The full moon lighted our way, and the riding light of Hesper [anchored near Thetis] furnished a mark to steer by. Mr. Teague woke up Mate Redman with a jab in the ribs and Capt. Hale with a shout, after which a series of arm pumpings followed. The twin-screw launch chugged away with Mr. Teague, all of us voting Teague a royal host and prince of good fellows. At midnight all was still on board Thetis, while the moon kept anchor watch for us.

[July 21. By Crosby. Thetis sails from North East Harbor to Rockland, a distance of 47 miles, in eight hours and nine minutes.] On this day we enjoyed the best sailing of the cruise to date, a smoky sou'wester keeping all sail pulling, and the lee scuppers awash much of the time. [A visit to town after supper, a "ripping game" of 63. All hands aboard and abed by 11:30.]

[July 22. By Foster.] At 4:30a.m. Bos'n Crosby awakens from his last night's sleep on Thetis for the season of 1910. Crosby's departure makes our feelings akin to the weather: gray, gusty and dreary. It is hard to have a shipmate leave. All hands wish the bos'n a most successful career with the Bell Telephone Co. [They sail for Port Clyde, arriving at 1:30] after a smashing sail to windward. Capt. Hale tacks ship and "the old lady" behaves handsomely. [They go ashore in search of milk.] Mrs. Hupper, aunt of Roscoe Hupper, kindly gives us three quarts of sour milk. Later F. Redman and A. Gould go ashore and with better luck return with milk and ice.... At 8:30p.m. supper is served consisting of a rich cake made from the sour milk. [Amid thunder and lightning a game of 63, followed by "arguments against girls' colleges".] At 10:45 we drink grog to the departed bos'n. At 11:20 Redman winds the clock and the crew silently wrap their mantles about them and pass into the land of nod.

[July 23. By Hale. Following breakfast and a game of 63] grog is served, all hands drinking to the health of Mr. and Mrs. Albert T. Gould. [Gould having announced his engagement.] At 11:50 F. J. Redman and R. Hale set A. T. Gould ashore. The three dangle their feet over the edge of the steamboat wharf, munching pears and whittling chips.... It is with sincerest sorrow that the members of the crew thus say goodbye to another of their number. But they are glad that the second mate...could be with them for even so short a time. [They sail to Boothbay, arriving late afternoon, in time to welcome Gould's replacement Robert Dillingham Morss of Portsmouth, New Hampshire, a Bowdoin classmate of Hale's.]

[July 24. By Redman. A quiet day in harbor, with trips to town for ice cream and mail. Achillles continues to sulk.] After dinner Capt. Hale and A. Randall work on the launch for an hour but she refuses to talk to us.... The captain and F. Redman row down to Mouse Island and make a most pleasant call on Mr. and Mrs. Allen Johnson. All hands return to Thetis at four bells and have supper.... All hands sit on deck, but no arguments are started. We go below and write letters. Mate Redman goes ashore with mail at nine o'clock. The fog has come in and the bell on Burnt Island and the whistle on Cuckolds can be heard.

[July 25. By Foster. Another day in Boothbay Harbor, spent playing 63 and debating whether to sail away to the west toward Massachusetts. The captain opts to remain where they are.] Redman somewhat disgruntled at not going to sea, throws himself off the main boom nearly splitting himself in two pieces. [By nightfall the wind has picked up,] halyards rattling and water swashing up against the sides. Moon slowly creeping out of the east. Harbor lights dance merrily and we feel much more comfortable than if we were outside [the harbor] with Redman "seeing what she could do in a breeze of wind".

[July 26. By Morss.] This bright morning Capt. Hale calls all hands at 6:40. After a breakfast of kidney beans the crew turns to and washes the decks and polishes the brass.... At 8:32 Thetis weighed anchor and filled away on the port tack. [By noon they are off Small Point. At 2:30 they sight a whale.] For supper we enjoyed one of Skipper Randall's most excellent cakes, which made, when eaten with maple syrup, a sumptuous meal. [They sail on through the night, Hale and Morss standing the first watch.]

[July 27. By Hale.] The wind clouds which had hung overhead during the previous watch were dispelled by the rising moon, and the rest of the night was brilliant as the day. The breeze freshened about one, and Thetis headed S[outh], ...logged off the miles in fine style. To one lying to leeward fo'ard, she seemed a boat all of silver plunging on alone through the glistening night.... Pass a number of vessels going into Boston, an English liner, a sloop yacht, a long tow, and a West Indies tramp. [They drop anchor in Provincetown harbor at 11:12a.m.]

After anchoring, all hands but A. Randall go in swimming. [One of the very rare occasions when Hale takes the plunge. It must have been hot.] It is unanimously agreed that the water is of a very pleasing temperature. A. Randall and R. Hale dine aboard in state at 1 o'clock, while the other members of the crew go farther and fare worse on a shore dinner. They return about two with the mailbag well filled. Read and write letters until 4:30 when R. D. Morss and R. Hale go ashore for stores, etc. On their return at 6, supper is served. More letter reading and writing.... The glass which climbed to 30 at midday went back to 29.90 by dark. Sky becomes overcast and threatening.

[July 28. By Redman.] ...After writing letters, the crew, all save skipper Randall, go ashore and climb Provincetown Monument. For nearly half an hour we enjoy the view from the top looking down on to... the fishermen anchored in the harbor as we would toy ships in a pool....

[July 29. By Foster.] The fog of the night hung thick in the harbor, so thick and black that we could not see the shore. Horns constantly announce the movements of some vessels. Glass 30.5, a steady 30.5, a steady upward crawl. No breeze astir. [After breakfast] decks washed down, then all hands fall to reading a favorite book.... R. Morss and T. Foster visit the Louisa Sylvia and look over the Josephine De Costa.... At 1 o'clock dinner is served. [The fog lifts.] Altho' the bay is motionless...the Costa and other vessels get underway; 18 men hauling on the throat halyard of Costa's mains'l. Reading and sleeping occupy the afternoon until 5 when all hands go ashore. [Back aboard for supper and 63, during which "Foster climbs and Redman sinks."]

[July 30. By Morss. More fog, along with rain showers. "Capt. Hale decides to lay at anchor for another day." A trip to town; several games of 63.] After supper was held an animated discussion on shipping subsidies and American shipping. This was followed by another game of 63. Grog was served at 9:30 o'clock, after which all hands turned in after a short discussion of the various merits of American poets.

[July 31, 1910. By Hale.] Day dawns with a good breeze which relieves our fog-smothered hearts. Glass at 29.88. Turn out at 4:30 as the sun is rising over Highland light. Under way at 5, [their destination Hyannisport.].... Obtain much amusement watching two whales playing to leeward. Wind cants aft. See a large turtle near surface of the water. Pass Chatham buoys at 12:10. Mate Redman gives us lobster stew for dinner.... Pass a great number of vessels bound North and sight a fleet of seven battleships a dozen or so miles off shore. [They reach Hyannisport at 8:45.] After everything is tied up, A. Randall calls for'ard for a good mug up. This repast is much appreciated by the crew. Turn in at four bells of a fine starlight night.

[August 1. By Redman. A day ashore, tending once again to the ailing Achilles.] At sunset everything is in readiness for an early start round the Cape tomorrow.

[August 2. By Foster. His account of their twenty hour voyage to Marblehead is a vivid one, reproduced here at length as evidence of the crew's hardy seamanship.] Crew called out at 3 o'clock, good breeze SW. Under way at 3:22. Short hitches out by breakwater until Thetis will make her course. Pass Bishop and Charles [buoys?] 4:30, at which time eastern horizon is tinged with fire of rising sun. Breakfast at 5:45. At 5:55 we pass red buoy on Handkerchief Shoal and start sheet. Jib tops'l out 6:10. Club tops'l at 6:20. Wind cants more southerly. Fog hangs in the distance. Pass Pollock Rip light ship 7:35, bears southwest. Start sheet again and run off for Pollock Rip Shoals light ship.... Jib tops'l taken in at 7:40. Six lumber laden three-masters are beating down over the shoal with the strong fair tide.... Pollock Rip Shoal passed at 9:19. Wind light.

At 10:48 whistling buoy off Chatham bears west. Breeze freshens, cants in to southwest. 12:55 Nauset lights bear west. A dinner of "schoush" [?], a mixture that sticks and fills. Hauled close. At 2:37 Cape Cod light bears west. Breeze freshens.... At 4:06 Race Point light bears south. Have a splendid sail over to Boston light ship; about sunset thunderclouds bank up in the north, and the sun throwing its last shafts abroad tinges the west and north with pink, rose, and purple.

Pass light ship at 7:45. Log 152 miles. Take in jib at 7:55.... Breeze good. Many steamers going east and west; a gigantic trans-Atlantic liner loomed up on our weather [side], making a particularly impressive sight. Lights of the North Shore shine in the distance. About three miles from harbor, breeze leaves us. At 10 o'clock another air springs up from southwest. Make Marblehead Rock, then haul to for an anchorage in harbor. At 11:05 drop anchor.... Glass at 30.22. Crew turns in immediately after drinking grog.

[August 3. By Morss.] Eight o'clock found the crew of Thetis ready for breakfast. A beautiful morning, hot with no wind stirring. After breakfast launch was lowered that Thetis might be moved further up the harbor, as she now lies on the starting line of the Corinthian Yacht Club. Launch, however, "strange to say," refuses to go. So mate Redman tows Thetis, rowing the launch. [The crew goes ashore in the afternoon] and before returning visited Abbott Hall and viewed A. H. Willard's "Yankee Doodle," a wonderful portrayal of American patriotism and personal character. [Foster brings his mother and a friend aboard.] They stayed for half an hour and pronounced themselves quite pleased with Thetis.... The crew spent the larger part of the evening sitting out on deck watching the numerous lights in the harbor. Grog was served, following on some of Redman's famous watermelon which he purchased ashore.

[August 4. By Hale. Following a morning sail to nearby Gloucester harbor, where they anchor for the next three days,] all hands turn to with a will to scrub and paint, [the start of a marathon two-day spruce-up. Foster returns from a trip ashore] and takes a dizzy drop from the heights of society, as represented by a touring car... to the depths of vulgarity, as represented by a piece of sand soap. Scrub waist, waterways, and outside of boat and also the tender. Through about six, when a magic transformation occurs of four paint scrubbers into genuine summer men. Mate Redman, T. A. Foster, and R. D. Morss dine at a chop suey joint on Main St., while R. Hale visits the Hawthorne Inn. Later the crew reassembles at the Inn and go to a dance at the new casino. But as T. A. Foster does not do the "Spanish" the evening is to be considered a failure....

[August 5. By Redman.] Day dawns fair. Wind WNW increasing as we begin to paint the outside of Thetis. Both sides are covered with fresh paint in the course of the morning....

[August 6. By Foster. A day spent provisioning and polishing brass.] All hands dress for dinner and dance at Hawthorne Inn. On this occasion, R. Morss shone the brightest.... <u>Special record</u>. The much despised Achilles thumped himself into our good graces during the morning in the following way: The sloop Pellegrina from Philadelphia was endeavoring to change her berth and the sailor in a rowboat could not tow her to windward fast enough to keep her from going afoul of the East Gloucester docks so Capt. Hale offered to hitch Achilles on, a bold offer, under the circumstances. Strange, but Achilles tugged like a good fellow, and we put Pellegrina in a satisfactory berth.

[August 7. By Morss.] Today, Thetis, resplendent in her new coat of paint became a great social centre [sic]. Crew arose at 7, and after breakfast set to work polishing brass. At 9 o'clock R. Morss and T. Foster went ashore for laundry. About 9:30 Capt. Hale and F. Redman set out in Achilles towing the rowboat for Hawthorne Inn, returning with Mrs. and Miss Rollins [Hale's grandmother and aunt], miss Margaret Moggill, Miss Elwell, Miss Holder, Miss [S?] and Miss Mann. [They sail offshore throughout the day, returning passengers to the Hawthorne Inn by 6.] Little Miss Margaret Moggell, but 12 yrs. old, was voted to be the brightest and most entertaining of the party. Her little stories were most amusing. [Was he joking?] Supper was served at 6:40 after which the crew swapped yarns. Following this the crew read and discussed poets until two bells, when grog was served and all hands soon turned in.

[August 8. By Hale. They set sail northeast toward home.] ...Many whales appear about us coming up occasionally to within a quarter mile. They occupy all our attention as they roll sluggishly. A splash, a spurt, a snoring sound, then a long, glistening line of black and they are gone, to come again within a minute. They have an air of comfort as they loll about in the smooth, calm sea. 11:15, ...scarcely a breath of wind but the day glorious and clear. Five minutes later the water broke under the lee fifteen feet away, and a dirty grayish back unrolled itself, then, scared at the close presence of the boat, dove instantly in such a way as to cross her bows diagonally. Each of us waited for the shock of a collision, but the great beast went clear.... [By afternoon the wind has died and Thetis lies becalmed, short of her destination for the night: Portsmouth. Achilles manages to tow them part way there but at 8:50 sputters out.] Anchor at 9:00 about half way between Whaleback and Portsmouth Light in 8 fathoms in mid-channel... a game of 63 in which R. D. Morss and R. Hale show Mate Redman and T. A. Foster the way to the finish. Rations of grog after the game. Night calm and very starry....

[August 9-11. Thetis is confined to Portsmouth harbor by foul weather. Trips to town and frequent 63 matches help pass the time. Redman departs for Ellsworth by train.]

[August 12. By Hale. The day "breaks fair", and the crew set sail for home. With no trouble they reach] Portland Head with breeze freshening at 4:45. Run up to House Island, take in headsails and pick up mooring at 5:00. Tie up sails and cover them. Take in colors at 5:53 and the cruise officially ends. Then comes a grand period of turmoil and confusion as the crew pack up below. By 6:30, all hands go ashore, sad to think that the eighth annual cruise has followed its seven predecessors into history.

Hale continued to sail Thetis with Lon in and around Casco Bay for the remainder of the summer, as he had in past years. And, with Morss, he ventured on a shorter "Eastern Cruise" in late August. Summing up the year on September 24, shortly before boarding ship for his first year at Oxford as a Rhodes Scholar, Hale wrote with evident pleasure that Thetis had that day completed the 6,146[th] mile of her history. "And in every mile she has demonstrated good qualities. She has never leaked a drop, never failed to work at the touch of the wheel spoke, never failed to stand up and smile when the wind blew and the sea came aboard." He wrote as well in praise of the crews, whose presence "accounts for the best of the season's pleasure." As he had at the end of other seasons, he pondered the future. "There are signs that never again will the activity of the Cushings Island fleet be as great as it has been the four years past. The old crew are still hopeful, however.... Meantime let the precious memories of 1910 mingle with the wealth of the past. This log has but tried to hint at the doings of the year which are vividly retained in the minds of their participants."

Hale's end-of-season entries in succeeding years were much as that one: praise for Thetis and her crews; hope that the happy times together would continue to make precious memories. In 1911 he declared, almost defiantly, that despite a shorter season, the log's chronicle proved "there are still bright days and fresh breezes, and hearts that love the sea". (RH XI, 116) The following year he consoled himself with the thought that though the log's brevity might "make sad reading...the old traditions are better maintained even if the splendours of a youthful past cannot be restored". (RH XII, 90. Soon after leaving Oxford, Hale adopted English ways of spelling.) At the end of the 1914 season, Thetis's last under Captain Hale, he was left to declare simply that thanks to the logs which he had maintained so lovingly, the first eight years of the good ship's life "are all destined to a durable and affectionate memory". (RH XIV, 93)

By that time, Hale had learned to cloak himself in memory as insulation_against the new and unexpected. He had begun writing poetry while at Bowdoin, often adopting the meter of his fellow Portlander, Henry Wadsworth Longfellow. Once at Oxford, he started to copy his efforts into his journal. On January 22, 1911 after only a few months in England, and yearning for the New England winters of his past, he drew on memory to declare his devotion to the kingdom he had, through his years of sailing, created for himself.

O sing me a song of the snow on the hills
Three thousand miles away,
For there is my soul and my whole heart thrills
at the thought of a vanished day.
O the unspecked white in the flare of the sun,
And the laden spruces dark
That straggle by bravely one by one
Where the rest of earth lies stark.

And I yearn again for the sounds of the wold
For the crunch of the trodden snow,
For the muffled murmer 'neath ice's hold
Where the nameless brooklets flow.
O what of the stretch of the open field

That the north wind sweeps across,
And the stone walls buried or half concealed,
And the white house grown with moss?

And speak of the isles in the winter seas
Of low suns o'er Manan's rock.
Is the snow piled high in offshore leas?
How spins the weather cock?
Does the wind blow East and the sky lower grey?
Comes snow from the sea tonight:
Have the gulls flown out to meet the day
Or lingered in harbours light?

Then when ye have told of the fields and hill
And the isles of the open sea
Speak on and tell of the forest chill
And the lake frozen solidly,
And the village set by the river's brim
And the glitter of frosty stars;
For here am I in a world made dim
By murk and the battle scars

Of man's long strife with a conquering time.
The pall is drawn; no breeze
To thrill a burdened soul to rhyme,
But visions from overseas
And the quickened stir of a yearning heart,
The thoughts of long ago
When my childhood's self played the hero's part
The lord of a world of snow.
(RH X, 400)

In the Land of Romantic Innocence

Can we call Robert Hale a Romantic and an innocent? And if we can, what does it matter? We could agree that his logs and journal provide a charming look into a world now vanished; and leave it at that. But something more can be drawn from them: more about Hale, and more about the way the life he describes evokes the time and place of his youth.

Hale certainly never called himself a Romantic. Instead he enjoyed declaring that he was a puritan. And in a sense, he was. Once, while visiting an Oxford friend, Richard Elkins, in London, he was surprised and displeased to discover a roomful of lady smokers. "They all sat about and smoked," he confided to his journal, "a performance I confess completely shocked my puritanic upbringing. The more I see of things," he declared, "the more contented I am that I am puritan." (RH X, 36-37)

Probably Hale would have been closer to the mark had he described his upbringing— and himself—as unworldly, rather than puritanical. Nevertheless, he certainly possessed a ferocious work ethic, worthy of the sternest pilgrim divine, frequently prepared to call down wrathful pronouncements upon his own errant laziness. "I have frivoled and frittered," he wrote to himself after his first six months at Oxford, where he was studying law. "Never before have I so played the prodigal with time. The fallacy I have committed is so absurdly fallacious—the fallacy of supposing one can have rest without toil, recreation without labour, play without work." (RH X, 152) During the weeks before his second-year examinations, he drove himself so hard that he came close to a breakdown. All of this evidence of a powerfully self-critical strain inside him. Yet a good puritan was expected to rein in emotions, not celebrate them. And Hale, in both prose and poetry, declared himself eager to let the world understand and sympathize with emotions that drove him far more insistently than any self-restraining puritanism would allow.

Hale was a Romantic because he preferred to see the world as he wanted it to be, rather than as it was. During his first year at Oxford, having just finished *Madame Bovary*, he confided to his journal that his dislike of the novel stemmed from the fact that Flaubert "chose to be the photographer rather than the painter." (RH X, 152) Hale was ever the painter, intent on pictures that allowed him to live in a world conceived to his liking, pictures deriving their subjects from life, certainly, but by no means entirely lifelike. He took to writers like Stevenson, Longfellow, and Kipling. During his years at Bowdoin, he had fallen under Stevenson's spell. "For three years he has been coming to this place in my intellect and affections," Hale wrote; now he was "more nearly like a flesh-and-blood friend" than most of his college acquaintances. (RH V, 39) And as his friend, Stevenson could lead him into a world of imaginings: life lived as Jim Hawkins lived it; life, that is, romanticized to project a highly personal gloss on a painting that might otherwise remain no more than one of "unvarnished" truth. It was the world conjured by Albert Gould in the 1910 log as he recalled "spinning toward South West Harbor, where picnic baskets and picnickers were lined up on the float": a world of "many fair women and brave men." (RH IX, 60) Gould's tongue may have brushed his cheek as he tried his own hand at picture-painting. Yet knowing Hale, he in all likelihood understood how his account would appeal to his friend's Romantic nature.

When the foreground figures in these paintings were not the fair and the brave whom Hale knew from college, from Cushings Island or Marblehead, they were the stalwart folk encountered when ashore Down East, and later during his travels on the Continent while on vacation from Oxford. His journals from these years contain dozens of "sketches" of European men and women who serve him in the same way the inhabitants of Harrington and Port Clyde did.

As a tourist, he saw himself a collector – of the quaint, occasionally of the grotesque. The people he described were an expression of what Europe at that time was to many rich Americans who traveled there: a cultural artifact, an "abroad" distinct from "home," a civilization that spoke only in the past tense, as a collection of objects to be studied and, for the most part, admired, rather than one to be encountered and then engaged with as contemporary.

Hale the artist fills the pages of his European journals, as he did his accounts of Down East life, with scenes and characters that helped him create the world he wanted to inhabit. He knew enough of painters to see that world through their eyes. While in Bellagio, during the spring of 1911: "Somehow this Italian sun is an artist after the manner of Titian, while in France I believe he is of Corot's school. There he is gay but never dazzling. Here he is brilliant. He is not content to ply the brush lightly. He must paint it all as in a dream, an exuberant fantasy of colour." (RH X, 194) Hale's landscapes – whether of Paris streets or Swiss Alps – were rendered to display the best in both man and nature.

At the corner of the Place de la Concorde there awaited me the finest bit of urban landscape I had ever seen. A clear mass of sky behind the chestnuts of the Champs Elysées glowed with the light of the departed sun. The dome of the Grand Palais was outlined against it. To the left a heavy thundercloud looked ominous save on its under edges where the twilight turned it to buff. The Eiffel Tower was a veritable thing of beauty very dim against the cloud. (RH X, 174-175)

[At half past three] we went for a stroll to the northeast up the Valley of the Isère [near Grenoble] …. As we turned to go home...the range of the Belledame turned to a faint rose with sunset tinge and the sky grew yellow…. Pink filaments of cloud floated overhead and the evening stars shown steadily from above the end of the valley. In a few minutes the mountains had grown dead again, like coals that had smoldered and gone out and we walked home in darkness. The evening, however, brought more pure radiant moonlight to shine upon mountains and valley. Who shall describe it, but who should fail to feel? (RH, XVI, 105)

That last sentence, surely, a fine distillation of the Romantic spirit.

On his first excursion to the Continent from Oxford, with a fellow American Rhodes Scholar, James Boyce, Hale immediately declared himself again the "artist." "Boyce is distinctly the sociologist of the expedition. I the student of still life. So it was to satisfy his desire that I went to the theatre of St. Malo." No sooner has he taken his seat, however, than he begins the mental sketch that he will later transfer to the journal. "The primitive theatre was crowded with folk: whiskered military, cheap looking women, fishermen and peasant girls with their white caps. One of them especially interested me. She sat watching eagerly from a front seat in the pit and her Celtic face might well enough have bespoken an Irish maiden." (RH X, 41)

Throughout the European journals Hale allowed his imagination to play over the faces and lives of the men and women he encountered and was happy to welcome into his world. Several had been dead for centuries. An archaic "youth" in the museum at Delphi, "looking very Egyptian with his broad shoulders and tapering waist. His rather stupid face wears a wholly Egyptian expression. He has been very little moved by the twenty-five centuries that separate [us] from his marble embryo." In Amiens, above the cathedral doors: "The kings of France, eleven feet tall, stood above us and gazed with pride over this fair land of theirs....They have had some seven hundred years longer to think things over than we have, and I suppose they have their very solemn convictions...but like all great monarchs they keep their own counsel and never have confided their opinions to one another." In Bologna, an ancient pew minder at the cathedral who appears to Hale more than ready for eternity. "An old woman I found warming herself over a pitiful little brazier showed me in... and I felt very sorry for [her] for she should have been tucked comfortably into a grave long ere this and the atmosphere in which she lived was not good for her." In the Pyrenees, a lively parade of gypsies that, when viewed from afar in the company of performing bears and two somersaulting monkeys, "were pleasing to my eyes," part of the human comedy he so enjoyed assembling and celebrating. (RH XVI, 267; X, 168; XVI, 197; X, 319)

As was the case in Maine, Hale preferred to people his landscapes with sturdy country stock. On that trip to the Pyrenees in the winter of 1912, he and a Canadian friend from Oxford lodged for a night in the tiny village of Luz.

It is of narrow streets and low houses and the only monument is the church, walled and fortified it is said by the Templars, and certainly by men of old who fought and worshipped in these Pyrenean fortresses. In the streets move the sturdy peasant men with their blue tam o'shanters, and bright-eyed, pretty peasant women and laughing jovial peasant boys. The kindest folk I know. [The following day they allow a carriage driver and his friends to talk them into a trip through the mountains to nearby Gavarnie.] The bystanders being accomplices, added remarks judiciously here and there. "Tomorrow," they said, "it will surely snow; today the mountains will be clear." We listened with interest. At last the driver got down and his eloquence took on that touch of the confidential which is always the ultimate device of the orator. "For 10 francs," he said, "I will take you." The tariff was 20. There is no argument like a good trade. "Done," we said, and with bows for all the natives we set off. Peasants in the village saluted us, and we bowed in return, feeling like monarchs in a royal progress. At a cottage higher up, a little boy ran out to pull off his cap. And peasants traveling to and fro with laden donkeys greeted us with cheerful smiles and pleasant greetings. [Once at Gavarnie, they sat down] to a lunch of omelette and tea in a bit of a café. Whither came all the village as we finished our meal. The men were all immaculate in collars and ties, and all were wearing their tam o'shanters. The boys too were dressed in a manner becoming the Sabbath, but strange though it seemed in good spirits notwithstanding. So we sat and ate in that bare room with all the peasants and talked of France and of mountains and of honest peasant life.... (RH X, 323-327)

By declaring himself a student of still life rather than a sociologist, Hale avoided the need to look beyond individual character and setting into broader landscapes. Harrington, Maine, once full of shipbuilders and fishermen, now all but destroyed by the precipitous decline of the coastal fishing industry, is to him simply an appealingly "decayed old town with a deserted and sleepy appearance in its streets." (RH IV, 354) Inhabitants who in the past might have sailed the seven seas, now compelled to dig clams for a living, were to Hale not the victims of relentless economic change, but heroes worthy of an ode. "Thou humble toiler of the ooze and mire," he declared to such a laborer, soon after arriving at Oxford in 1910,

Industrious, plodding, steadfast and content,
Is not they sturdy back to labor bent
As worthy of a poet's lyre
As age-old stories of the fire
Of love that flamed in Daphnis's heart or rent
With lusting Thyrsis for some maid who spent
The nights communing with Selene dire.
I undervalue not thine honest hoe
To shepherds' crooks, and count thy reeking toils
Upon the wavering verge of sea and land
As fair a labour as the landsmen know
Who spend long days in gossip or in broils.
Thy soul is clean, though mud be on thy hand.

(RH X, 15)

On his journeys throughout England and Europe, he continued to fill his world with those whose sturdy backs and clean souls fed his own Romantic soul, lifting them from their own worlds and into his. Through that process, he could avoid thoughts a sociologist or economist might have found themselves compelled to confront. As his train carried him through the bleak countryside of England's industrial midlands on the way to the Lake District in late April, 1912, having noted that "the month might easily be June save that the vales had hardly yet come into full leaf," he continued, "the country through which we passed was industrial in character, so that in spite of the beauty of the day and season, the general effect of the scenery was none too pleasant." And that was that. (RH X, 364)

Only once, in all the hundreds of pages of logs and journals, does Hale find himself forced to take a photograph rather than paint a picture. The result terrified him. In June of 1911, he traveled to London to witness the festivities surrounding the coronation of King George V. On Coronation Day, June 22, he left the home of his Oxford friend, Richard Elkins, making his way to his allotted seat in a grandstand facing St. Margaret's Church alongside Westminster Abbey. Throughout the morning he watched as officers marched, bands played, and carriages drove up "freighted with the wealth and nobility of England." Finally the procession: "The magnificent state coaches with their liveried footmen and outriders. But beyond the glory of the men," Hale declares, "was the glory of the horses, the finest specimens of that noble animal I have ever seen." At last, the king.

As the monarch drove by, the band played "God Save the King," and the people went into a modest fury of applause. It was, indeed, a modest fury. The English boast that their controlled natures will never permit those revolutionary and unrestrained fits of passion which mark the history of the French. But neither can they demonstrate any such responsive enthusiasm. In France or in America, a ruler could not get so mild a tribute of approbation.

Following the ceremony, Hale "joined the crowd in vulgar stares at the peers and peeresses....The magnificence of their costumes was beyond the imaginings of most people. But in beauty of countenance, they were not in any sense distinguished."

Thus far, Hale's description was not unlike a great many of his "pictures": painted with deft strokes, providing a lively sense of England's Vanity Fair in which the distinction of carriage horses far surpassed that of peers and peeresses. And then, very suddenly, there is a change. Forced to walk back to his friend's house in St. John's Wood, he crosses St. James's Park.

There, and in front of Buckingham Palace, the horror of it all came upon me. I had seen squalor before. I had seen it in Naples, poverty and filth and misery. But in Naples, somehow, it is relieved. There is music and sunlight and gaiety in the heart of the wretchedness. But here there were hundreds of thousands of humankind pent up in a dull, gray, prison city, the dregs of the populace whirled for the moment to float on the top of mankind. And what a contrast to the brilliance of a few moments ago. There was the world in epitome in a brief half hour. Here in the Park they were lying and standing about, dirty and bedraggled, speaking a strange unintelligible dialect of their own. It was hard to see why they were burdened with existence. I could not see that life gave them joy. And yet this was their holiday. There was no poetry, no picturesqueness in their poverty, no beauty in the deadening monotony of their existence, no capabilities of happiness in their misshapen bodies, dwarfed minds and stunted souls. And so it made one shudder as he passed amongst them into the troop that was surging back up the Edgeware Road.

I was tired when I got to the Elkins', but tea and a nap revived me, and at seven, accompanied Richard and "Bill" Mathers to Garrick's Theatre. The play was Kismet, a fantasy of incidents in the Baghdad of a thousand years agone. As a play it was certainly amusing. As a pageant, it was the finest I have ever seen. For the Orient was before you, its mosques, its beggars, its bazaars, the sunshine, the simplicity and the magnificence of its life. But ever and again as the play went on, there came to our ears in the theater the noises of the tragedy of life which was going on without and which no walls could keep from us. And when our little play was over, there were the other players in the street, a million of them it seemed, howling and whirling in the streets. And they smelled to heaven with the stench of beer, reeking of the most unlovely places of earth.

It was a relief to get through them to a house, a bed, and rest.

(RH X, 235-240)

Just this once the world comes crashing in. Hale could make a place for the "poetic," "picturesque" poverty of Naples, but not for this "howling, whirling" nightmare. Though distracted for a couple of hours by the romance of "Baghdad of a thousand years agone," he could not escape for long the dreadful reality of here and now, those incessant "noises of the tragedy of life" so close by. It is a measure of his success in keeping the world at bay that when it broke in upon him, it devastated him so shockingly.

Fortunately, Hale was scheduled to board ship for home two days later; he could console himself with the thought that another summer sailing with old trusted friends lay before him. As the years passed, while he remained steadfast in his devotion to Lon, those friendships came to include a circle of contemporaries, particularly his faithful crew member Fulton Redman. That his emotions were strong and that he was eager to express them is further evidence of Hale's Romantic nature. Nineteenth century Romanticism was about many things; it was certainly about emotional attachments: between men and women, but also between two men—the kind of "manly" friendship that Tennyson celebrated in his tribute to his dead friend Arthur Hallam, "In Memoriam." Hale wrote two poems about Redman, the first dated Oxford, October 19, 1910, soon after he arrived in England. Its title: "Summer's End. F.J.R. August 10, 1910," the day Redman had left the cruise to return to New York and his job with a law firm. It is written as if by Redman and ends on an elegiac note, since Redman assumed – incorrectly as it turned out – that his work would keep him from future summers aboard Thetis. Hale's melancholy stanzas expressed his own sadness at the loss of his friend's companionship.

> I hear the breakers coming to the shore.
> The pounded beach is drumming with their
> roar.
> But I will hear their drumming nevermore.
> (RH, X, 16)

The second poem, written in Berlin on January 15, 1911, though it does not mention Redman by name, is nonetheless a tribute to him and to the closeness Hale felt toward him. Hale imagines himself before St. Peter, struggling for evidence of worthy deeds to gain admittance to Heaven, and finding none.

> So turned I sadly from the Heavenly steep,
> Looked from celestial brilliance to the night
> That hung about our lower world so deep.
> And then as one who hidden gold hath found
> I turned upon the angel with a shout
> Till all the upper heavens echoed 'round
> "I had a friend," I cried. And turned about.

(RH X, 134)

Whether or not Hale ever read these poems to Redman, his accounts of their conversations leave no doubt that they were conscious of and grateful for the friendship that lay between them. In 1913, after Hale's final year at Oxford, he and Redman sailed Thetis together for a week, with Elmore Randall, Lon's brother, as the only other crew aboard. Thy reached Pemaquid after a day's sailing. "My soul drank in contentment," Hale wrote in his journal. "I talked to Fult about the inimitable joy of sailing a boat, the joy that obliterates the years and annihilates cares and kills ambition. He understood me. We were both very happy." Two days later they were content to be wrapped in fog, with nothing to do but enjoy each other's company.

The fog, as Fult said, had taken the last vestige of ambition from us and left us happy because helpless. To me it seemed so necessary to the melancholy beauty of this outpost harbor [Round Pond]. When are the weather-beaten barn and the somber pines on the bleak point so lovely as when the swift fog softens the backgrounds and makes all a harmony of vague, pensive gray? No sort of weather is so sympathetic, so expressive as the sea fog....These are some of the things Fult and I talked [of] as we walked....The wet beat upon us but we were never happier. For the rest of the day we sat below and wrote and talked and read. And time never passed quicker. It was bed time before I realized it. (RH XVI, 379-381)

After four more happy days, Redman left Hale and Thetis for New York.

Fult left at six in the morning. It made me lonely and unhappy to see him go. Three years ago he had left in the rain at Kittery [the occasion for Hale's poem] and we both thought our sailing days were over. He has been back for three trips since then and I bless him for it....These trips are melancholy without the matchless exuberance of his personality.

Recalling the trip after he returns to Cushings Island, Hale laments Lon's absence but proclaims that "Fult's presence – which is as necessary as Lon's to make a cruise a joy – Fult's presence we had, and we prized it."

He then adds: "These cruises are no longer vital joys. They have a sacramental value, to recall the treasured past of our youth and the memory of the sea. So do Fult and I regard them and I am sure that we are right." (RH XVI, 390) Hale is saying that rather than continuing to create new pictures, he and Fult are by now blessed instead with the ripe pleasure of recollecting the scenes they have painted together in the past. "Is it not wonderful," he had asked himself five years before as he perused an album of Cushings Island photographs, "that in the sight of some old pictures, comes flooding back upon us the memories of years?" (RH V, 11) Now, the memories had themselves become those pictures.

Hale well understood that memories could be a source of pain as well as pleasure. He acknowledged this to himself when writing of Lon's stroke earlier that same year. "I have built up the fabric of reality on...memories," he cried out in his journal, "and now every tentacle of thought aches with indescribable pain." (RH XVI, 175) Yet Hale had no reason to believe that the world his Romantic nature had helped him bring to life, despite its occasional aches, would fail him as he moved forward into manhood. Largely unacquainted with what lay outside that world, he could not imagine a time when he might no longer be able to reach out for reassurance and support to the memories that were, as he realized, the fabric of his reality.

At the end of the Second World War, Walter Lippmann, one of America's leading public intellectuals, wrote an essay about his country's role as world leader in the coming years. In it, he argued that until the twentieth century the United States had lived in a state of innocence.

When I attempt to compare the America in which I was reared with the America of today, I am struck by how unconcerned I was as a young man with the hard questions which are the subject matter of history. I did not think about the security of the Republic and how to defend it. I did not think about intercourse with the rest of the world, and how to maintain it. I did not think about the internal order of the nation, and how the needs and the work of our people were to be kept in balance with the resources of the nation....In my age of innocence I thought that the struggle for existence had long since been happily concluded.

The "effortless security of the decades after the Civil War," Lippmann continued, had produced "the exceptionally private character of American life" that was its hallmark until the First World War. Americans believed they could live safely apart from the rest of the world, sheltered by geographical separation, but – equally important – by their sense of themselves as special, almost providential. (Walter Lippmann, *U.S. War Aims*. 1944, 196, 204)

Hale, born just two months after Lippmann, expressed this sense of America's isolation as he bid farewell to the old world following his last trip to the Continent from Oxford in the spring of 1913. "I could see very well into the future. For a year

I shall glory in America, its enthusiasm, its liveliness, its energy. The old world will hold very little place in my thoughts and sympathies. Then the longing for it will come on….When this yearning comes, I hope I can satisfy it. Otherwise life becomes really discontented." (RH XVI, 325) Europe was one place, the United States distinctly another, too isolated, he feared, to permit him the satisfaction of a trans-Atlantic citizenship.

One paid a price for isolation – at least if one was saturated in European culture as Hale now was. Its great advantage, however, as Lippmann pointed out, was that it permitted "innocent" young men like Hale to ignore the world's misfortunes while enjoying the fruits of America's insular prosperity and progress. Hale's innocence was further insured, of course, by his determination to encase himself in that Romantic world he so enjoyed painting. It was all but guaranteed by the geographical isolation in which he grew up. Had he been raised elsewhere, in New York City, perhaps, he might have been compelled to come face to face with the kind of "photographs" his romantic imagination shunned, while weighing the evidence that Jacob Riis's real photographs of New York City slum life was placing before the eyes of Americans willing to look.

Four years of college at Bowdoin, less than fifty miles from home, did nothing to challenge his innocence. In one of the few journal entries he wrote during those years, he evinced a contentment not unlike that he experienced during summers Down East.

It has been for me a pleasant Fall, one of joyful reunion and renewed associations. I have worked harder than ever before in my studies, but I have walked many a mile in the cool Fall air, through woods and across the plains to the sea….And in these walks I am never at a loss for a good companion. Indeed, with the advent of sophomore year, I feel that my friendships have become stronger and more numerous….As the day of Thanksgiving is at hand, and the eighteenth anniversary of my birth, I feel sincerely and devoutly thankful for the benefits and bounteousness that have attended not merely these last two years but my whole life. (RH V, 35-36)

Hale's three years at Trinity College, Oxford, though more challenging academically and socially than those spent at Bowdoin, continued to bundle him away from the world. The university did all it could to ensure his isolation from the bustling town around it. During the day, when he ventured outside the college gates, he wore a cap and gown that encouraged locals to steer clear. At night, regulations enforced by university proctors required him to be back inside the college and locked away from the world by ten. There was a good deal of drunken rowdiness among the undergraduates – Trinity was notorious for it – but it almost always took place inside the college walls, was childish in nature –"innocent" fun, and as such largely tolerated by the authorities.

All this isolation did not prevent Hale, enthusiastic Romantic that he was, from falling in love. But his brief affair – if it can be called that – was as much as anything an expression of the innocence that was so much a part of his nature. On his first vacation from Oxford, in December, 1910, while in Paris, he looked up a family of very distant cousins: Professor and Mrs. George Ellery Hale, their son – and their daughter Margaret. (The fact that she shared her name with Robert's much-loved mother must have struck him as an astonishing and significant coincidence.) George Hale was well on his way to acquiring his reputation as a world-renowned astronomer. Robert, who initially spent time exploring Paris with the professor, soon turned his attention to Margaret. The family left the city briefly. On their return, Margaret and Robert saw more of each other and began to enjoy an easy companionship. "She and I played cribbage for some time and afterward talked: she very seriously and prettily, I whimsically but much in earnest." When the George Hales left Paris in early January, Robert confided to his journal that "they are the most agreeable acquaintances I have made [since coming abroad]. And I believe that one of them at least has emotions quite as strong as my own." (RH X, 101, 104)

Yet the difference in their ages weighed on Hale's mind. And no wonder. He had just turned twenty-one; she was thirteen. Later in the month, Hale expressed his continued attraction, and his confused reaction to it, in a poem.

> I love thee that thou art a child
> And more that thou'st a woman grown.
> But which thou art so unbeguiled
> And yet so womanly I own
> I cannot tell. But this I know
> That when we met I felt alone
> In all a hemisphere, but lo,
> Henceforth the loneliness was gone.
> But soon thou too wert gone away
> Forever, as I thought, until
> There came an undreamt fairer day
> And once again I searched thine eyes
> To learn from their sincerity
> The wherefore of this love that lies
> Within my heart so stubbornly.
> And even then I could not tell
> Nor better now, so I must wait
> And wait and think, and think me well –
> But even then I fear I cannot tell,
> For such is fate.
>
> (RH X, 130)

It reads like a chapter from a Victorian novel: they meet, sense a bond; yet realizing the impediment that lies between them, part and go their separate ways. So romantic the attraction; so innocent the love that emerges from it. That, at least, was how Hale appears to have seen it. Had that novel been written, its final chapter would have described the couple's wedding day five years later, and sent them off on their happily-ever-after life. In this case, a few letters back and forth between Oxford and Pasadena, where the Hales lived, and that was that: fair, innocent maiden; ardent, equally innocent swain. Finis.

By 1913, Hale's final year abroad, Europe was edging toward catastrophe. If he did not recognize the fact, he was of course not alone. His journal contains the unconscious ironies one finds in similar accounts of those years, many written by his English counterparts. Hale's American innocence may simply have increased his ability and willingness to overlook what, in hindsight, appears obvious. In January, 1913, he attended a New Year review of troops while in Grenoble.

The soldiers were out in their thousands, marching and counter-marching and doing all manner of things to which my military vocabulary does not extend. They did not look at all like the erect and uniform lead soldiers I used to play with, and still less like the German troops which always excite my laughter....They all looked quite normal human beings, very good humored and bright and wholesome. They took to their maneuvering in a far more vivacious manner than the Germans, thus entirely escaping the ludicrous appearance to which I am accustomed from soldiers. (RH XVI, 137)

The following month he went with a friend to an airplane show at Olympia Stadium in London.

It was my first opportunity of inspecting at close range these still novel contrivances. They looked extraordinarily matter of fact standing there on their wheels or runners in the vast building. Here were big and little ones all colors and sizes, byplanes [sic] and monoplanes with every variety of ingenious contrivance for propellers and rudders. One or two had little guns but these looked strangely toy-like. The wings spread over light ribs were made of oiled canvas like the covers to an eights boat [rowing shell]. They seemed frail, to say the least. (RH XVI, 167)

Back in the United States for good in 1913, Hale continued to study law at Harvard for two further years, then took up practice in Portland. Though Thetis had been sold, he and Redman, now married, nonetheless continued sailing Down East for several summers. On August 6, 1916, they weighed anchor at the start of the fourteenth annual cruise aboard Redman's boat Polly. Two days out, in Mackerel Cove, near Ellsworth, the sailors anchored for the night. Hale recorded a supper of soup, succotash and blueberries. Rain began, but aboard "good ship Polly" all was contentment. "A snug harbor, the patter of raindrops and friendliness below decks add to the quota of human happiness....Captain Redman reminiscent of Ellsworth's seamen and ships aforetime." (RH XV, 51)

In France, meanwhile, the Battle of the Somme entered its second murderous week. Within a year Hale would be in uniform. One recalls Philip Larkin's poem, "1914," and in it his oft-quoted epitaph for those who marched off to war in the years after 1914: "Never such innocence." Never, indeed.

Afterword

This is the way the world ends,
Not with a bang but a whimper.
(T.S. Eliot, "The Hollow Men")

Robert Hale's private world — the world we have watched him create — had come to an end by the time the First World War was over. Certainly not with a bang; Hale never fought in the trenches on the Western Front, or anywhere else. And just as certainly, not with a whimper. Though he lost his innocence, he managed to hold on to the optimism that had been its corollary. From the fragmentary evidence available — a packet of letters written to his mother from France — Hale's world appears to have ended by degrees, until one day there was simply nothing left of it.

In May, 1917, a month following America's entry into the war, Hale commenced a frustrating, six-month attempt to get himself to France, first as an enlistee in a Harvard-sponsored ROTC regiment, then as an artillery trainee at Ft. Monroe, Virginia. Eventually, he turned to his cousin, Fred Hale, at that time a congressman, who arranged for his almost immediate embarkation as a regimental sergeant major, leapfrogging him ahead several grades in rank from private. Once overseas, he was rapidly commissioned a second lieutenant, shifting from one job to another until he found himself the junior officer in an agency – the Board of Contracts and Adjustments – with responsibility for settling claims and approving contracts between the American Expeditionary Force and its allies.

To what extent Hale had angled from the start for a desk job, to what extent the obvious wire-pulling was initiated by him or by others – his parents, perhaps – there is no way of knowing. Hale was twenty-eight years old and a lawyer. Perhaps it's best to agree that his age and talents made him a more useful combatant behind a desk than on the front lines.

He sailed for France on a United States Line ship. (Security regulations prevented his telling the family which one.) Just like old times, he reported to his sister Katharine, as he enjoyed the pleasures of an almost pre-war-like crossing. "How nice and 'shippy' everything smells and how courteous and obliging the stewards are." His letter is evidence that he was crossing the Atlantic with his Romantic self fully intact. "Everything I see," he declared exuberantly, "fills me with admiration for the two great nations of the world – the British and the French. I pray that our own race shall be numbered with them, and that together we shall inherit the Earth." (To Katharine Clifford, 12/26/17. RH Misc.)

Hale disembarked at Southampton on Christmas day. The following night he crossed the Channel in a horse transport, sleeping – and not sleeping – in the open, with the temperature between 10° and 20° above zero. For the next two days he traveled to Paris in a troop train at ten miles an hour, stopping for the night at a "rest camp" where he slept with eleven others in a tent pitched on snowy ground, "huddled together in a vain attempt to stay warm." By the time they reached Paris on the evening of the 28th, they had "been in our uniforms for a week and had not had a wash for three days and four nights." A hot bath and decent meal at the YMCA revived him. And off he went following what was almost certainly the most unpleasant forty-eight hours he had ever spent in his life. (To MH, 12/30/17. RH Misc.)

Not enough by itself, certainly, to compel him to cast aside the past. But a beginning. His letters to his mother over the next ten months until the Armistice were at first cheery, then increasingly less so. Little is more deadening to the soul than the routine of Army bureaucracy: the monotony, uncertainty, and triviality of it, despite the undoubted necessity of it – all this took its toll.

Don't for a moment fancy my life as anything but a civilian's. I wear a uniform. But I eat civilian meals, think civilian thoughts, sleep in a civilian bed....We are simply lawyers and businessmen. I am fitted for the work and do it measurably well. But frankly I hate it. I mean I hate this sedentary indoor life of ease and luxury. I had no idea it would be so difficult to stick to a non-combatant life. As things are now, I shall [have to] indefinitely." (To MH, 7/13/18. RH Misc.)

That was in July. Three months later, he wrote again of his unhappiness. He asked his mother and father to understand that his desire to get himself to the front lines was not "animated by a foolish love of adventure on the one hand or an exalted patriotism on the other." Those Romantic notions no longer compelled him as they once might have. "It is simply a very powerful impulse to be as your fellow men are....It is as fundamental as a child's impulse to walk and talk." A month later he reported that he had finally arranged reassignment to a replacement division. "This means I shall be sent to some school for further training and go hence to the front." A week later the war ended, along with any hopes Hale might have had of joining his fellow men in combat. (To MH, 10/7/18; 11/4/18. RH Misc.)

He remained at his desk in Paris until March, 1919. At which point he was surprised and pleased to find himself attached to a mission to investigate conditions in the Baltics, where Soviet and rogue German forces threatened to destroy the already flimsy chance for peace.

We are just going to see that the Bolsheviks are Bolsheviking as they should, and that all the little Trotskys really trotsky. I know you won't be pleased at the news, but I have not done anything but sedentary jobs yet, and probably won't in the next forty years, and I look forward to it frightfully....Forgive me, and don't worry because I wasn't born to be killed by Bolsheviks, and shan't be. The trip is what I want to do, and though I am a complete cynic as to the value of missions of this kind, I think it will be interesting to look back on and tell the State Street [church, in Portland] Guild about. (To MH, 3/28/19. RH Misc.)

Whether he ever appeared before the ladies of the Guild, he did report his adventures to his fellow Rhodes Scholars in a thoughtful though light-hearted article he wrote in the July 1920 issue of *The American Oxonian*: "War and Diplomacy on the Baltic."

Though Hale may have remained dubious about the success of military missions such as his, the cynicism he expressed to his mother did not make him the less hopeful for the future. But that hope was expressed in language stripped of the flamboyant patriotism he had exuded while on the trip over to France – his prayer that the Allies might inherit the earth. Now his fear was that America, in its new position of world leader, would prove as materialistic as he believed the Germans had been. "If there is anything as ignoble as men slitting each other's throats, I think it is the merciless and ruthless pursuit of money and material riches. I wish I thought America were cured of it, but I suppose she isn't." In a subsequent letter he again expressed his fears: "History will take the course that the passions of men give it."

And yet, he added, "I believe in the League of Nations and every device new or old which might lessen war." (To MH, 10/7/18; 1/12/19. RH Misc.)

Somewhere along the way, Hale seems to have emerged from his pre-war world into this new one, where reasonable men and women, once they had brushed illusion from their eyes, might prove themselves capable of working for a better future. In a letter to his mother in the summer of 1918, without his recognizing it, he appeared to be declaring a final independence from his old Romantic self. "I want to be a Garibaldi or at least [General] Georges Foch, who sits near me at a café every now and then, his breast covered with well-earned medals. But I realize that I am Hale and neither Foch nor Garibaldi. Sometimes it is nice to be yourself. Other times you feel it is a very disconcerting limitation." (To MH, 7/7/18. RH Misc.) Nice or not, accepting one's real self – Hale as Hale, not as Garibaldi or Foch – that acceptance would, he hoped, enable him to live his life as he now wanted to.

Within three years of his return home, having bid farewell to his world of Romantic innocence, he began a career of public service that culminated in his eight terms as a Maine congressman. America, as Walter Lippmann would argue, was coming of age as well. It makes sense to suppose that Hale hoped the work he was undertaking would assist in a transformation that would bring his country to its own maturity.

On August 1, 1920, Hale, Fulton Redman, and Albert Gould set forth on the sixteenth annual cruise. They sailed aboard a rented sloop for just a week, the only additional crew being a chef, Mr. Hopkins, "formerly of the Vanderbilt menage, it is rumored." It was to be their last recorded sail together. On their second day, they anchored in Point Lookout Harbor, then proceeded to climb "Mt." Lookout, elevation 586 feet.

There are two vantage points on the summit, the one covering Penobscot Bay, the other Mt. Desert Island and Blue Hill and Jericho Bays. The islands lie spread out as from an airplane. We counted eighty-eight....Of course the view, especially toward sundown, is delightful. What surprised us most was York Island Harbor to the East'ard almost unmarked on the chart but sheltering apparently in perfect security some fifteen of sail and fishing sloops. (RH XV, 97)

In past accounts Hale would at that point, in all likelihood, have written of times past — or rather, "times agone"; of friendship, of memories. But there is none of that now. We can, if we choose, imagine those three men thinking such thoughts, saying either much or very little. We can imagine them as well speculating a bit about the future. Or taking a look back, if only to say, in the words Robert Graves chose for the title of his war memoirs, goodbye to all that. That Hale had said goodbye seems clear enough, from those letters to his mother and from what he does not say on the occasion of the final cruise. Even though he never fought on the western front, he was close enough to that tragedy to have absorbed it and to have allowed his knowledge to transform him.

In further confirmation of that conclusion, these two pieces of evidence. First, Hale's marriage: In 1922, aged thirty-two, he married Agnes Burke, a successful short-story writer at work in New York City. Agnes was a quick-witted, often sharp-tongued Irish Catholic, born and raised in New Jersey. In her Cushings Island memoir, "Summers I Remember," she declared forthrightly, "I was a dedicated Manhattanite. Everything west of the Hudson, and east perhaps of Westport, Connecticut, I considered the frontier, the sticks, the backwoods. New York, then as now, teemed with young people like me who had come there to breathe the sharp air of a metropolis." (Agnes Hale, CIM, 31) It says something of Robert that he was able to persuade Agnes to come live with him in the shadow of his formidable family in remote Portland, Maine. It says as much if not more of him that he chose her to marry. No one could have been further removed from the society of those "fair maidens" who had flirted innocently on the piazzas of the Hawthorne Inn and the Ottawa House in the days before the war. No proposal could have more eloquently declared Hale's emergence from the world of his youth.

The second piece of evidence: Never once in the memory of those who knew him in middle age and beyond, do those friends recall him setting foot on a boat, other than the ferry that carried passengers back and forth to Cushings Island. Nor do they recall conversations about times spent aboard Thetis. Whether recollections of that life brought pain and sadness with them, whether they simply seemed irrelevant to the life he now led – perhaps some combination of the two – who can say? Clearly, though, at some point he decided to shut out that part of his past. In his youth he had resolved "before all and through all" to be a seaman; time and experience had compelled him to forgo, if not forget, that resolution. Eventually he gave away his sailing charts to a much younger Cushing Islander. We can be thankful that he never threw out the logs and journals. By keeping them, he left us a picture – a painting – of his life within a world that can, as we read of it, give us pleasure as well.

Appendix

Robert Hale's Crewmen

<u>Thomas Bosworth</u> (Mermaid cruise, 1906). Born in 1888, Bosworth moved east when eleven to live with his grandmother, first in Portland, then in Cambridge, Mass. He was a member of the Harvard class of 1910; upon graduation he went, along with Hale, to Oxford as a Rhodes Scholar. He joined the staff of the *New York Times* in 1915, where he worked until 1935, with the exception of time spent in France with the American Field Service during the First World War. His career after the *Times* remains something of a mystery. At one point he worked for the Burns detective agency in Washington, D.C. In 1953, Hale arranged for his appointment as assistant doorkeeper of the U.S. House of Representatives. He died in 1957. (Source: *Portland Press Herald,* October 8, 1957)

<u>John Leland Crosby</u> (Thetis cruises, 1909, 1910). Crosby, born in 1888, was raised in Bangor, Maine. He was a member of Hale's class (1910) at Bowdoin. Throughout his adult life he worked for the New England Telephone and Telegraph Company, in Boston, Springfield, Mass., and Orono, Maine, where he died in 1983. (Source: Bowdoin Directory)

Sumner S. Fogg (Thetis cruises, 1907, 1908). Born in 1887, Fogg grew up in Portland, Maine where his father was a wholesale druggist. He does not appear to have attended college. He is listed in the 1930 U.S. Census as a salesman, married and living in Brookline, Mass. (Source: Ancestry.com)

Thomas A. Foster (Thetis cruises 1907, 1908, 1910, 1911). Foster was a member of the Dartmouth class of 1910. He attended Harvard Medical School and served with the Harvard Red Cross unit in France during the First World War. He practiced medicine in Portland until his death in 1967. (Source: Harvard Directory)

Albert T. Gould (Thetis cruises 1909, 1910, 1911, 1912). Gould was born in Thomaston, Maine in 1885. He attended Harvard but transferred to Bowdoin, where he graduated summa cum laude in 1908. He received his J.D. from Harvard and practiced law in Boston throughout his adult life, specializing in admiralty law. After spending a summer in Labrador as secretary to the Grenfell Mission, founded to assist needy families there, he and Sir Wilfred Grenfell remained lifelong friends, Gould frequently assisting Grenfell with legal matters. He died in 1947.
When awarded an honorary degree by Bowdoin in 1946, Gould was described as a "lover of the sea and loyal friend of men who have gone down to the sea in ships." (Source: Bowdoin Directory)

Robert Dillingham Morss (Thetis cruise, 1910). Morss, born in 1889, was a member of Hale's Bowdoin class. He worked throughout his life for Ginn and Company, publishers. He died in 1940. (Source: Ancestry.com)

Fulton Jarvis Redman (Thetis cruises 1907, 1908, 1909, 1910, 1911, 1912, 1913). Native of Ellsworth, Maine, born in 1885, Redman was four years older than Hale. He graduated from Bowdoin in 1907 and from Harvard Law School in 1910. Unlike his friend, Redman was a life-long Maine Democrat. He ran three times for U.S. Senate and once for Governor, losing all four contests. He was publisher of the *Portland Evening News*. He died in 1969. (Source: Wikipedia and Bowdoin Directory)

Acknowledgements

My thanks go first to Howard Dana, Robert Hale's great-nephew and the owner of Hale's logs and journals. This book would not have come to life without his generous, loyal support. Thanks as well to my indefatigable typists, Toni Palter and Dwight Spears; to my tech-savvy associate Adam Palter; to Shirley Quinn, my meticulous copy editor; to Jim Anderson, for his fine map; and to Peter Murray and Peter Plumb, for sharing their knowledge of sailing and of the Maine coast.

Further thanks to the following, for various contributions: Dorothy Browne and Jan Reid, Dagmar Hamilton, Olive Hershey, Sarah Hitchcock, Donald Lamm, Sarah Meacham, Becky More, Tim More, John More, Nick Noyes, David Percival, Jamie Rice, Will Russe, Laura Sprague, Earle Shettleworth, Manfred Wolf, and Paul Woodruff.

At iUniverse, George Musialik proved time and again that in this age of impersonal, and occasionally frustrating high technology, the reassuring professionalism and patient counsel of a human being can make all the difference in the world.

About the Author

Standish Meacham is Sheffield Centennial Professor of History, Emeritus, at the University of Texas at Austin. He is the author of five books dealing with the social and cultural history of nineteenth and early twentieth century England. He was also co-author of the W.W. Norton textbook, *Western Civilizations*. Since 1961 he has spent summers on Cushings Island in Casco Bay, where he became friends with Robert Hale toward the end of Hale's life.

Printed in the United States
By Bookmasters